ENGAGING WORLDS

Core Texts and Cultural Contexts

---

*Selected Proceedings from the Sixteenth Annual
Conference of the Association for Core Texts and Courses
New Brunswick, New Jersey
April 15–18, 2010*

Edited by

**Robert D. Anderson
Molly Brigid Flynn
J. Scott Lee**

University Press of America,® Inc.
Lanham · Boulder · New York · Toronto · Plymouth, UK

Copyright © 2016 by
University Press of America,® Inc.
4501 Forbes Boulevard
Suite 200
Lanham, Maryland 20706
UPA Acquisitions Department (301) 459-3366

10 Thornbury Road
Plymouth PL6 7PP
United Kingdom

Library of Congress Control Number: 2016937695
ISBN: 978-0-7618-6796-8 (paperback : alk. paper)
eISBN: 978-0-7618-6797-5

™ The paper used in this publication meets the minimum
requirements of American National Standard for Information
Sciences—Permanence of Paper for Printed Library Materials,
ANSI Z39.48-1992

Contents

Part II. When Cultures Meet

Part III. Modern, Postmodern, and Future Horizons

Part IV. Challenges from Core Texts

Part V. Political Worlds and Worldly Politics

Part VI. Moral Images of Humankind

Acknowledgments

We are grateful to the following for permission to reprint various extracts, listed by the chapter author:

Brewton:
Excerpts from "The Cultural Mediation of the Print Medium," by Michael Warner, reprinted by permission of the publisher from THE LETTERS OF THE REPUBLIC: PUBLICATION AND THE PUBLIC SPHERE IN EIGHTEENTH-CENTURY AMERICA by Michael Warner, p. 17. Cambridge, Mass.: Harvard University Press. Copyright©1990 by the President and Fellows of Harvard College.

Fisher:
For permission to reprint from Perelandia and Till We Have Faces, by C. S. Lewis:
PERELANDIA by C.S. Lewis copyright © C.S. Lewis Pte. Ltd. 1944.
TILL WE HAVE FACES by C.S. Lewis copyright © C.S. Lewis Pte. Ltd. 1956.

Flynn:
Extracts from *Aristotle's Political Theory: An Introduction for Students of Political Theory* by Richard Mulgan, reprinted by permission of Peters Fraser & Dunlop (www.petersfraserdunlop.com) on behalf of Richard Mulgan.
Thanks to University of Chicago Press for permission to reprint excerpts from:
Hannah Arendt, The Human Condition. Chicago: University of Chicago Press, 1958
Aristotle. The Politics. Trans. Carnes Lord. Chicago: University of Chicago Press, 1984, 2013
Alexis de Tocqueville. Democracy in America. Trans. Harvey C. Mansfield and Delba Winthrop. Chicago: University of Chicago, 2000.

Hall:
Extracts from "The Fate of Pleasure" from THE MORAL OBLIGATION TO BE INTELLIGENT: SELECTED ESSAYS by Lionel Trilling. Farrar, Straus and Giroux, June 2000.

Kamber:
Excerpts republished with permission of John Wiley and Sons Inc. from *Free Will*, ed. Robert Kane, 2002; permission conveyed through Copyright Clearance Center, Inc.

Kauth:
CEREMONY by Leslie Marmon Silko © 1977, 2006 by Leslie Marmon Silko. Used by permission of Viking Penguin, a division of Penguin Group (USA) LLC.

McGovern:
Small Wonder: Essays by Barbara Kingsolver, © 2002 HarperCollins Publishers.
Prodigal Summer by Barbara Kingsolver © 2000 HarperCollins Publishers.

Mackey:
Excerpt from "What I Believe" from TWO CHEERS FOR DEMOCRACY by E.M. Forster. Copyright 1939 by E.M. Forster. Copyright renewed 1967 by E.M. Forster. Reprinted by permission of Hougton Mifflin Harcourt Publishing Company. All rights reserved.

Meinke:
Excerpts from NIGHT by Elie Wiesel, translated by Marion Wiesel. Translation © 2006 by Marion Wiesel. Reprinted by permission of Hill and Wang, a division of Farrar, Straus and Giroux, LLC.
Nairn:
Willa Cather, My Antonia, 1994; used with permission from Dover.

Roney:
157 words (pp. 94, 27, 294) from FATHERS AND SONS by Ivan Turgenev, translated by Rosemary Edmonds (Penguin Classics 1965. Reprinted 1975). Copyright © Rosemary Edmonds, 1965. 'Fathers and Children,' the Romanes Lecture 1970 copyright © Oxford University Press, 1972. Reproduced by permission of Penguin Books Ltd.

Sagan:
Hampton Press for permission to reprint excerpts from Mind and Nature: A Necessary Unity, by Gregory Bateson, 2002.

Shmikler:
EICHMAN IN JERUSALEM : A REPORT ON THE BANALITY OF EVIL, by Hannah Arendt, copyright © 1963, 1964 by Hannah Arendt, copyright © renewed 1991, 1992 by Lotte Kohler. Used by permission of Viking Penguin, a division of Penguin Group (USA) LLC.
Excerpts from ESSAYS IN UNDERSTANDING, 1930-1954, by Hannah Arendt. Copyright © 1994 by Harcourt, Brace, & Co. Reprinted by permission of Houghton Mifflin Harcourt Publishing Company. All rights reserved.
Excerpts from THE LIFE OF THE MIND, Volume 1, by Hannah Arendt. Copyright © 1978 by Harcourt Mifflin Harcourt Publishing Company. Reprinted by permission of Houghton Mifflin Harcourt Publishing Company. All rights reserved.

Westervelt:
Excerpts from The Zohar : Pritzker Edition volume 3, trans. Daniel C. Matt, copyright © 2005 by the Zohar Educational Project, Inc. All rights reserved. Used with the permission of Stanford University Press. www.sup.org.
Jewish Publication Society, for selections from Legends of the Bible, vol. 1, by Louis Ginzberg, 1956.
Excerpts from The Book of J by David Rosenberg and Harold Bloom, copyright © 1990 by David Rosenberg and Harold Bloom. Used by permission of Grove/Atlantic, Inc. Any third party use of this material, outside of this publication, is prohibited.
Augsburg Fortress, for permission to reprint excerpts from Genesis 12–36: A Continental Commentary, by Claus Westermann (Trans. John J. Scullion), © 1995

Introduction

The theme of the Sixteenth Annual Conference of ACTC and the title of this volume of selected papers—"Engaging Worlds: Core Texts and Cultural Contexts"—centers on two hallmarks of education rooted in core texts. First, a text-based, core-structured education aims at breadth and is thereby intrinsically horizon expanding. Core texts cross all disciplinary boundaries and bring their readers into contact with diverse worlds—some real and others ideal; some possible and others unattainable; worlds lost, worlds at hand, and worlds still in the mists of futurity; some forgotten, others ignored, and others still firmly in consciousness; worlds imagined, felt, deduced, intuited, revealed, created, and deconstructed. Thus, the conference committee asked attendees to consider: "What are the worlds and cultural contexts of the activities and agents constituted in core texts?"

A second hallmark of a core-text education flows from the first. Intimate familiarity with core texts and with the variety of vistas they offer makes liberally educated students more at home when abroad. Wherever they go, whatever their walk of life, little they encounter will be completely new to them. Engagement with flesh-and-blood human beings in all their diversity and with this world in all its complexity comes more readily to students who have lived in the many worlds encountered in core texts. Thus, the conference committee asked attendees also to consider questions such as: "What is the relationship between core texts and citizens in a democracy?" "What can classic works—ancient and modern—contribute to the formation of institutions?" Can great books "not only engage us with our own present culture, but cultures of another order altogether?"

Conference attendees were invited by the conference committee to "engage in as wide a conversation based in core texts as did the committee that formulated the theme." The invitation was accepted. In fact, the sixteenth conference was the largest in the history of ACTC to that point. Participants came not only from North America, but also from Asia, Europe, the Middle East, and South America. Papers dealt with core texts from all continents, and discussion was rich, diverse, and plentiful.

The papers have been arranged under six rubrics and in six sections. The first section includes papers that describe and advocate for various intellectual strengths as one of the desired outcomes of core-text education. These intellectual virtues include clarity, sophistication, self-awareness, nimbleness, flexibility, judgment, and precision and accuracy in expression. Each of the papers in this section also addresses a critical aim of core-text education: to draw students across the divide from intellectual bystanders to intellectual participants. In the second section, four papers consider what are the lessons to be learned when the cultures of peoples clash, and a fifth intriguing paper considers what emerges when, aboard Melville's ship the *Pequod*, the culture of slacking meets the culture of work.

The first of the two middle sections of this volume corrals papers dealing with possibilities that emerge from contexts that are modern, post-modern, and whatever is forthcoming thereafter. The second of the two middle sections includes thought-provoking challenges from core texts—from a Laguna Pueblo story to *The Souls of Black Folk* to a "quantum narrative."

The concluding two sections of this volume consist of nine papers on the human worlds of political association and moral agency. The first group of papers explores the bonds of political community, the freedom of association, the political order presupposed by the good life, the political response to human depravity, and the inseparability of politics and economics. The second group makes the case that various core texts, especially novels and other fictions, can do two things. On the one hand, they can well convey things like the responsibilities of global citizenship and the complexity of real people and real human interaction. On the other hand, they can well counter things like the common belief that some of the worlds people have a foot in are moral free zones.

From the approximately three hundred papers delivered in New Brunswick, New Jersey, more than seventy were submitted for inclusion here. We thank all of their authors for the healthy competition that resulted. In the end, though many were submitted, only few could be chosen. We also thank our twenty reviewers from twelve different institutions who followed a blind review process to help us winnow down the submissions to twenty-nine selected papers. Reviewers include Peggy Pittas, Lyndall Nairn, David Freier, Anne Marie Flanagan, Jim Roney, Michael Dink, Kirsten Lodge, Alfred Martin, Don Marshall, Dan Murphy, Kathleen Kelly, Cynthia Wells, Edward Harpham, Monte Brown, Fr. John Fortin, Joe Spoerl, Matthew Konieckza, Max Latona, Tom Larson, and Phil Pajakowski. Finally, we thank our production editor Peggy Kelley and copy editor Jean-Marie Kauth for their steady and generous assistance in bringing this volume to completion.

We ask you to reflect once more on the final words of the conference committee's theme statement: "What do we learn of texts, cultures, and the world's dynamics when we read so widely and deeply? What books, what arts, what associations and institutions, what sciences, what religions, what cultures, what educations, what citizens, what scholars, are we preparing for the future through an education in core texts that engages our worlds?" Some answers to these questions are found in these selected papers. In the borrowed words of two of our authors, we hope that you find these selected papers hold "the power to intellectually provoke and inspire" and that you find in them a few of "those rare moments when words join together to form a lens that brings vision into focus."

Robert D. Anderson
Saint Anselm College

Molly Brigid Flynn
Assumption College

J. Scott Lee
Executive Director
Association for Core Texts and Courses

Part I. A Good Mind Is Hard to Find

Fate, Hope, and Clarity

Richard Kamber
The College of New Jersey
President, Association for Core Texts and Courses

Ralph Waldo Emerson liked to greet old friends by asking: "What has become clear to you since we last met?"[1] Knowing the cynical bent of *my* old friends, I am reluctant to tempt them with that kind of an opening. Still, it is an enticing invitation and one whose importance I have grown to appreciate. My predicament is not that I *lack* answers but that I have too many. More often than not, my mind is clouded by a stream of "on the one hand/on the other hand" considerations. So I prize those rare moments when words join together to form a lens that brings my vision into focus. My quest for clarity is professional as well as personal. As a teacher, I am continually seeking ways to make hard concepts intelligible to students. My aim is not merely to acquaint them with issues current in my field. I also want to help them appreciate why an issue is worth caring about and how it is connected to the best thinking and writing outside of my field.

These are hard time for higher education. According to the AAUP, salaries for continuing faculty members—when adjusted for inflation—declined for the first time since the early 1970s. Shrinking endowments and cuts in external support for higher education have forced colleges and universities to scour their budgets looking for programs to cut. Sadly, the ax of fiscal austerity falls all-too-often on the study of foreign languages and other limbs of the liberal arts. We have seen culture wars before, but what seems to be on the chopping block today is culture itself. The fact that higher education in the United States and Canada is one of the great success stories of the past hundred years is too often ignored by panicky pundits casting about for a quick fix to economic woes brought on by reckless pursuit of a fast buck. Yes, it takes time to learn how to think clearly and critically, and patience to become conversant with the best that has been thought and said. But these intellectual investments pay reliable dividends.

Given the uncertain state of the world's economy, the struggle of colleges and universities to make ends meet, and declining appreciation for the long-term value of liberal arts education, organizations like ACTC are bound to face tough challenges over the next few years. Do we have the strengths necessary to succeed? Although ACTC has little in the way of material assets, it has strengths of a different kind. Let me mention three. First, we have the dedication and enthusiasm of our members, volunteers, advisory board, and Executive Director. Second, we have a proven record of success in our conferences and projects. Third, we have a well-focused mission built on an educational philosophy that we know from our own classroom experience works for students.

These strengths constitute a potent combination, and we should be proud of them. But there is a difference between having these strengths and putting them to work. My first year of service as President of ACTC has made it clear to me that ACTC's continued growth and prosperity is built one email and phone call at a time. When I agreed to serve as President of ACTC, I told Scott I would spend whatever time the job required. "In for a penny, in for a pound," I said. Not surprisingly, the sum has turned out to be much closer to a pound than a penny, but I have been a little surprised by how many pennies it takes to make pound. We succeed because we invest time to make friends for ACTC, invite colleagues to present at a conference, convince administrators to sponsor or co-sponsor a conference or project, help write a grant proposal, put in a good word for ACTC at a grant-making foundation or at an organization like the Oxford Study Abroad Programme, work on the annual proceedings, and devote ourselves to many similar tasks. I believe that if we maintain this level of commitment, the future of ACTC is assured.[2]

One of the virtues of core texts is that they can provide memorable paradigms and points of reference for gauging the lucidity of our own reflections. Abraham Lincoln once told an admirer that in order to get a clear understanding on what it meant to "demonstrate a proposition," he interrupted his study of law and learned by heart the books of Euclid (Robinson 113). I like to think that my own field, philosophy, has a special role to play in the attainment of clarity. William James defined philosophy as "an unusually obstinate effort at thinking clearly."[3] What he meant is that philosophy persists in seeking intelligibility in the universe beyond the limits of inquiry that other disciplines set for themselves. James had no illusions about the difficulty of this quest or how often philosophers lose their way. He deplored the "the over-technicality, and consequent dreariness" common among philosophers in American universities. He warned that: "In a subject like philosophy, it is really fatal to lose connexion with the open air of human nature, and think in terms of shop tradition only" (James, *Pluralistic Universe* 637).

Here, then, is a puzzle. Although philosophy is supposed to aim at clarity, its practitioners often lapse into obscurity. A striking example of philosophy gone wrong is cited by Brand Blanshard in his elegant essay *On Philosophical Style*.

Listen to this from a great philosopher. I leave out only the first word and ask you to form the best conjecture you can of what he is talking about : "X is the self-restoration of matter in its formlessness, its liquidity; the triumph of its abstract homogeneity over specific definiteness; its abstract, purely self- existing continuity as negation of negation is here set as activity." You might guess the writer of this—it is Hegel—but I would almost wager the national debt that you do not have the faintest suggestion of what he is actually *talking* about. Well, it happens to be heat—the good familiar heat that one feels in the sunshine or around fireplaces. I strongly suspect that this farrago is nonsense, but that is not my point. My point is that even if it is not nonsense, even if a reader, knowing that heat was being talked about, could make out, by dint of a dozen re-readings and much knitting of eyebrows, some application for the words, no one has a right to ask this sort of struggle of his reader.

Barrett Wendell, in his admirable book on writing, points out that clearness and vividness often turn on mere specificity. To say that Major André was hanged is clear and definite; to say that he was killed is less definite, because you do not know in what way he was killed; to say that he died is still more indefinite because you do not even know whether his death was due to violence or to natural causes. If we were to use this statement as a varying symbol by which to rank writers for clearness, we might, I think, get something like the following: Swift, Macaulay, and Shaw would say that André was hanged. Bradley would say that he was killed. Bosanquet would say that he died. Kant would say that his mortal existence achieved its termination. Hegel would say that a finite determination of infinity had been further determined by its own negation (79–80).

I suspect philosophers are at their most obscure when they are least sure about what they want to say or why others should believe it. Even Hegel could be strikingly clear when he spoke about things close to his heart like freedom and world history. As a teacher of philosophy, I spend a good deal of time combing texts for concepts and examples that students can use to light their way through the darker corridors of philosophical arguments and counterarguments. Some of those I find come from philosophical texts; others from literature, history, science, or film.

One of the topics I discuss with my students is the free will debate. Unlike some problems in philosophy, this one has personal and practical implications. What we believe about free will and responsibility can make a difference in what we demand from ourselves and others. It can influence how we mete out praise and blame, reward and punishment. The free will debate is very old and notoriously difficult. In *Paradise Lost*, a band of fallen angels tries to reason through issues of "Providence, Foreknowledge, Will, and Fate. . . . And found no end in wand'ring mazes lost," though their "Vain wisdom" and "false Philosophie...excite Fallacious hope" (II.557–69; 245). If angelic intellects can't reach truth on these issues, it may be hubris for humans to think that they can do better. But philosophers are obstinate. Over the past forty years analytic philosophers have produced an impressive body of original work on free will, and some of it, though quite technical, seems to me worth sharing with non-philosophers. I propose to spend the remainder of this essay summarizing insights I have gained from reflecting on this work with the help of reference points drawn from core texts.

A good place to begin is with Robert Frost's deceptively simple poem, "The

Road Not Taken" (Frost). This poem can serve as a metaphor for the experience of choosing between alternative possibilities and as a way of illustrating traditional theories about freedom and responsibility.

The fatalist says that if you are fated to travel down one road rather than another, then doing so is inevitable. You end up on the road you are fated to take regardless of causal conditions. The determinist says the road you take is determined by causal conditions. You could not have taken the other road unless those conditions had been different. The libertarian says you could have taken the other road even if causal conditions had been precisely the same.

The most plausible argument for global fatalism is divine foreknowledge. If God knows infallibly what we are going to do before we do it, then no one could ever do anything that would render God mistaken. This does not imply that God *causes* our actions, but it does rule out alternative courses of action. If God knows you are going to take the road "less travelled by," then it would be impossible for you to take the road "more travelled by" (Henry Ford once boasted you can buy a model-T in any color you want as long as long it's black). Divine foreknowledge does not inhibit your doing what we you want to do, but it does entail that what you want do is inevitably the one thing that God has always known you were going to do. This nakedness to the eye of God may be discomfiting in its own right, but our worries become more acute when moral responsibility is at issue.

If God knows from all eternity that you are going to cheat on your income tax next year, then it would have be impossible for you to render Him mistaken by doing the right thing and not cheating. So, inevitably you cheat on your taxes. But who is to blame? It seems unfair to hold you responsible for failing to do the right thing when the right thing is impossible to do. Yet how can we blame God for your deliberate misdeed? He knew that you were going cheat and why, but he didn't cause you to cheat. St. Augustine's solution to this problem is unapologetically blunt. He argues that divine foreknowledge does not diminish in any way human moral responsibility. You are responsible for an action if it is caused by your own will rather than forced upon you by some external cause. If you cheated on your taxes because you willed to do so, then you are responsible. It does not matter that you could not do otherwise. All that matters is that you acted willfully.

To be sure, there are other ways to deal with the problem of divine foreknowledge. One can deny that there is a God or that God has foreknowledge. Boethius argued that since God is outside of time his omniscience is "of a never fading instant rather than a foreknowledge of the 'future'" (5.6; 64). What is intriguing about Augustine's approach is that it remains relevant to contemporary debates over the compatibility of determinism and moral responsibility. In most respects determinism is a far cry from divine foreknowledge. Determinism asserts that every event—including human choices and actions—is caused by natural conditions and law-like regularities. What this staunchly secular doctrine has in common with divine foreknowledge is that it rules out alternative possibilities. Everything that has ever happened and everything that will ever happen is the inevitable consequence of an unbroken chain of causes and effects. Under the precise conditions that obtained when you took the road less travelled many years ago or the conditions that will obtain when you complete your tax forms next April only one course of action is possible. The Principle of Alternative Possibilities asserts that we are not responsible for an action, unless we could have done otherwise. But determinism implies that we could *never* have done otherwise.

The ancient atomists flirted with determinism, but it did not become a mainstay of Western thought until the scientific revolution. Newtonian physics seems to guarantee that the motions of all bodies, including human bodies, are governed by universal laws that left nothing to chance or non-physical causes. To make room for free will, one had either to exempt human actions from deterministic laws or to reinterpret free will so as to make it compatible with determinism. Short of rolling back time, there is no way to tell whether a human being will always do precisely the same thing under precisely the same conditions. Although psychologists could set up a laboratory experiment in which a human subject was asked to make a simple choice over and over again under tightly controlled conditions, they could never be confident that the causally relevant conditions remain precisely the same. Humans are continually gaining new experiences and reassessing the old. The pre-Socratic philosopher Heraclitus probably had reality itself in mind when he said "we cannot step into the same river twice." His ontology is summed up in the aphorism *panta rhei* (everything flows). But even if *panta rhei* is *not* true of all reality, it is true of us. We are protean beings who do not remain the same from moment to moment. Continual learning continually changes who we are. We are, in the deepest sense, lifelong learners.

Writing at the end of the nineteenth century, William James pinned his hopes for free will on *indeterminism*. He urged voluntary belief in the seemingly untestable hypothesis that there is an element of chance in the workings of the universe. "What sense can there be," he asked, "in condemning ourselves for taking the wrong way... unless the right way was open to us as well...? I cannot understand the belief that an act is bad, without regret at its happening. I cannot understand regret without the admission of real, genuine possibilities in the world" (James, *Dilemma* 135).

Contrary to James's expectations, indeterminism turned out to be testable. Countless experiments performed in the decades after his death compelled physicists to conclude that probabilistic rather than deterministic laws govern the sub-atomic realm. At that tiny scale causal *in*determinacy—pure chance—plays a central role in the working of the universe and Newtonian mechanics gives way to quantum mechanics. Although skeptics have continued to nourish the hope that the role of chance in quantum mechanics will eventually be explained away by a deeper deterministic theory, indeterminacy has withstood nearly a hundred years of relentless testing. Experimental physicists are now exploring the extent to which indeterminacy operates at larger scales of physical reality. Double slit experiments with buckyballs—soccerball-shaped molecules made up of sixty carbon atoms—show the same wave-particle duality that has long been observed in much smaller particles like photons and electrons. Similar tests using viruses are being developed (Hawking 63–8). Experimenters have also found circumstantial evidence that quantum entanglement—where a pair of unconnected particles acts like a single system—may be involved in biological processes such as photosynthesis and the navigation of migratory birds (Vlatko).

What makes these experimental results important to the free will debate is that they falsify determinism at a scale of physical reality large enough to have the potential of bearing on human choice and action.

If quantum indeterminacy is to play any significant part in the exercise of the will, it must be through the neural operations of the brain. The libertarian philosopher Robert Kane has developed a theoretical model that piggy-backs on the shoulders of quantum physics to envision cases where human beings could have done have otherwise even if causal conditions had been precisely the same. Kane hypothesizes that in cases where powerful reasons and motives pull us in different directions so that we are deeply conflicted about which direction to choose, our internal uncertainty "corresponds to a window of opportunity that temporarily screens off complete determination by influences of the past" (Kane 228). In such cases, he thinks, one's will can tip the neural balance and "*make* one set of competing reasons or motives prevail over the others then and there *by deciding*" (Kane 228). It remains to be seen whether this hypothesis will prove compatible with the results of future research on what goes on in our brains when we make decisions, but even if it proves compatible with neural processes, philosophical objections still remain.

A frequent objection to Kane's model is that it gives us a picture of human choice-making that looks more like accidents than acts of volitions. Kane's response to this objection is that his model applies preeminently to episodes of inner struggle between competing reasons and motives, where the outcome will be a "self-forming act." He asks us to imagine a businesswoman who has to choose between trying to stop an assault and trying to keep an appointment that may be crucial to her career. Since she wants to go both ways, both are motivated, but being "one traveler" she must decide between them. "And when she succeeds in doing one of the things she is trying to do, she will endorse that as *her* resolution of the conflict in her will, voluntarily and intentionally, not by accident or mistake (Kane 232). Kane reasons that because the outcome of this conflict is not determined, the effort that succeeds in resolving the conflict and gaining her endorsement is truly "up to her." And he contends that such "self-forming acts" provide the basis for "ultimate responsibility." Insofar as future choices by this businesswoman are grounded at least in part on the character she has developed through this and other self-forming acts, she will be *ultimately* responsible for them.

My own objection to Kane's model is that it yields an anemic theory of free will and responsibility. It treats free will (self-forming acts) as the exception to the rule of determinism and presumes that we can make sense out of holding people responsible for their determined actions as long as we can trace their motives back to a self-forming act. But, as Jean-Paul Sartre points out in *Being and Nothingness*, self-forming acts are seldom one-time events (32–33, 433–81). The smoker who resolves in the evening to give up his habit for good, must face the same choice next morning. The smoker might wish that his prior resolution would relieve him of the burden of having to make that choice all over again, but it does not. The desire to smoke will take a long time and many agonizing moments of decision before it fades into memory. Similarly, if the businesswoman in Kane's example is confronted with the same tough choice at a later time, she may experience the same inner conflict all over again. One might say that Kane's model suffers from uncritical application of the "road not taken" paradigm. Few choices are hard-to-reverse decisions that "make all the difference." And the formation of character, as Aristotle understood, is a slow process of habituation achieved through practice.

Some appealing views on free will and character have been developed in recent years by philosophers who argue that free will and responsibility are *compatible* with determinism. One such compatibilist view has been crafted by Harry Frankfurt, a philosopher who is best known to the public these days for a little book—a very little book—entitled *On Bullshit*. Frankfurt essays on free will are not as easy to read, but he is a meticulously clear thinker and no bullshitter. He compares freedom of will to freedom of action. Just as freedom of action is the freedom to *do* what one wants, so freedom of the will is the freedom to *will* what one wants (Frankfurt 136). The phrase "will what one wants" is simple in form but requires explanation. I *will what I want* when the desires I have conform to the desires I want to have. A smoker who wants to give up smoking wants to get rid of the desire to smoke as well as the practice of smoking. Someone who wants to be more caring about the well-being of others wants to cultivate the desire to see others flourish as well as to perform specific acts that benefit others.

In short, Frankfurt treats free will as an achievement of character formation rather than as an innate human power, and he couples this with a view of moral responsibility reminiscent of St. Augustine's. Frankfurt argues that we are responsible for acts we do voluntarily even if we could not have done otherwise. He invites us to consider thought experiments such as the following. A devious neurosurgeon has planted a device in your brain that will infallibly cause you to cheat on your taxes. Because of this device it would be impossible for you not to cheat. But the neurosurgeon (being devious) has programmed the device so that it will not kick in if you cheat of your own accord. Now, let us suppose that you cheat of your own accord. You fail to report cash income. You estimate that the rags you gave to the Salvation Army are worth a $1,000. You declare your goldfish as a dependent. Since you cheat of your own accord, the device never kicks in. Should you be held responsible for cheating? (Most people say "yes," even though it is clear that you could not have done otherwise.)

Cases of this kind are called Frankfurt-type examples, and dozens of essays have been devoted to debating their merits. If nothing else, they have prompted a reexamination of the relation between moral responsibility and being able to do otherwise. Frankfurt-type examples tend to employ science fiction scenarios, but there are other examples that are more down-to-earth. Daniel Dennett cites the case of Martin Luther at the Council of Worms. When ordered to recant his (supposedly) heretical theses, he is alleged to have said: "Here I stand, I can do no other." Luther may not have spoken precisely these words, but *if* he did it is unlikely that he was trying to duck responsibility. It is not uncommon for people who perform heroic acts to deny that they could have done otherwise. Pawel Remba, a Polish Christian who smuggled Jews out of the Warsaw Ghetto, had this to say about himself and his fellow rescuers: "All of us looked at this help as a natural thing. None of us were heroes; at times we were afraid, but none of us could act differently" (Remba, cited in Tec 654). If being able to do otherwise is a necessary condition for moral responsibility, we should not praise people like Luther or Remba. But we do them praise them, and we do hold them responsible for their courageous actions.

Judgments of blame are trickier. People who have done blameworthy things often seek to excuse themselves by claiming that it would have been difficult or impossible for them to do otherwise. If I tell you truly that I failed to come to your house for dinner because I was hit by a truck or never received your invitation, it would be unreasonable of you *not* to excuse me. But not being able to do otherwise isn't always a reasonable excuse. In the *Nicomachean Ethics* Aristotle notes: "we punish a man for his very ignorance, if he is thought responsible for the ignorance, as when penalties are doubled in the case of drunkenness; for the moving principle is in the man himself, since he had the power of not getting drunk and his getting drunk was the cause of his ignorance" (Bk III, Chap 5; 113b. 30–35). This is a nice example, but we may wonder just what it means for the *moving principle* to be in the man himself or to have the *power* of not getting drunk. We seem to be back again at Kane's thesis that ultimate responsibility must be grounded in self-forming acts where one could have done otherwise.

Are there really clear-cut examples within the realm of ordinary experience where we blame ourselves, even though we know we could not have done otherwise? I believe there are. Suppose that last Tuesday you forget that you promised to pick up a friend at the airport at 2 PM. Indeed you didn't remember until 4 PM. If you had no alternative reasons or motives for going to the airport at 2, then I submit that it would not have been psychologically possible for you to do so deliberately. I also submit that you are likely to hold yourself morally responsible and blameworthy for failing to pick up your friend as you had promised to do. Of course, there may be an issue here about degrees of negligence. But let us suppose that you have always had a good memory for obligations of this kind and took reasonable precautions to remind yourself that your friend was coming to the airport. If you still blame yourself in spite of these precautions and the impossibility of doing something for which you had no reason or motive at the time, then you stand with Augustine and Frankfurt in believing that being able to do otherwise is not necessary for being blameworthy.

But if we lack the power do otherwise, what other power might we have that renders us appropriate subjects for praise or blame? Why do we hold humans but not animals morally responsible for their actions? An intriguing answer is suggested by an unlikely source. In the last voyage of *Gulliver's Travels* Gulliver gives his Houyhnhnm master a graphic account of the mayhem wrought by human warfare. The Houyhnhnm is horrified and says to Gulliver: "That although he hated the Yahoos of this country, yet he no more blamed them for their odious qualities, than he did a gnnayh (a bird of prey) for its cruelty, or a sharp stone for cutting his hoof. But when a creature pretending to reason could be capable of such enormities, he dreaded lest the corruption of that faculty might be worse than brutality itself."

This passage suggests to me that the power to reason might be substituted for the power to do otherwise as one's qualification for being held morally responsible. In fact, such a theory has been developed in considerable detail by Susan Wolf. She takes Frankfurt's thesis "that one's will is free when one has the desires that one wants" and adds that one's will is sane and responsible when it is governed by reality. She argues that to be truly free and responsible, we must also have the ability "to cognitively and normatively appreciate the world for what it is" and to correct ourselves accordingly (Wolf 156). The shift proposed here is profound. Wolf and Swift (as I read him) are proposing that the autonomy necessary for moral responsibility is more cognitive than conative. It is the capacities to learn, reason, and self-correct over time rather than the ability to do otherwise at the moment of choice that makes an agent worthy of moral praise or blame.

I do not pretend that this is the end of the story. There is much more be said about these notoriously difficult topics. However, I hope that I have succeeded in illustrating how insights drawn from core texts can resonate with arguments drawn from contemporary philosophy to help see us see more clearly appealing options for the resolution of dilemmas that touch our very souls.

Notes

1. This quote is also attributed to Benjamin Franklin.

2. I am happy to report that the Association for Core Test and Courses has had a very good year. Despite deep cuts to the budgets of college and universities, support for ACTC by individuals and institutions continues to be strong. Contributions to ACTC from institutional members have kept pace with last year. This year's conference—our sixteenth annual conference, "Engaging Worlds: Core Texts and Cultural Contexts"—is being sponsored by Seton Hall University and co-sponsored by Centenary College, Columbia University, The College of New Jersey, and The Richard Stockton College of New Jersey. Conference registration for the past two years has averaged 270; this year registration will exceed 300. Plans are already underway for our annual conferences in 2011 and 2012.

Thanks to ACTC board member Norma Thompson, Yale University has agreed to sponsor next year's conference. Carthage College has agreed to sponsor our conference the following year in Milwaukee, and Pepperdine University has indicated its willingness to fund the cost of a student conference in 2011.

I am especially pleased to note that beginning in 2010–2011, the Oxford Study Abroad Program (OSAP) will award a fellowship each year to a faculty scholar selected by ACTC to spend up to eight weeks in Oxford. To be eligible, applicants must be an ACTC member whose home institution is an institutional member of ACTC. Benefits include airfare (up to $700), housing (for up to eight weeks), assistance from OSAP office staff, affiliation with one Oxford College, library privileges, access to public lectures at all thirty-nine Oxford colleges, and free participation in all student field trips and excursions. We are grateful to Robert Schuettinger, the founder and director of OSAP, for this splendid opportunity.

As a result of the Advisory Board's decision to adopt term limits for Board members, two long-time members of the Board, James Woelfel (University of Kansas) and Michael Jones (University of Chicago), completed their terms in 2009. I am grateful to both for their years of service and look forward to their continued involvement with ACTC. The Board has also elected three new board members: Bruce Kimball (Director of the Education Department at Ohio State University), Mark Schwehn (Provost at Valparaiso University), and Grant Venerable (Provost at Lincoln University). Their names will be submitted for ratification to the membership of ACTC at the business meeting on April 18.

3. In *The Principles of Psychology*, James remarks "Metaphysics means nothing but an

unusually obstinate effort to think clearly." but he is using "metaphysics" to mean what most philosophers mean by "philosophy." See James (148).

Works Cited

Aristotle. *Nicomachean Ethics.* 18 July 2011. <http://www.sacred-texts.com/cla/ari/nico/nico027.htm>

Augustine, Bishop of Hippo. *On Free Choice of the Will.* Trans. Thomas Williams. Indianapolis: Hackett, 1993.

Blanshard, Brand. *On Philosophical Style.* Bloomington: Indiana UP, 1967.

Boethius. *The Consolations of Philosophy.* Ed. James J. Buchanan. New York: Frederick Ungar, 1957.

Frankfurt, Harry. "Freedom of the Will and the Concept of a Person." In *Free Will.* Ed. Robert Kane. Malden, MA: Blackwell, 2002.

Frost, Robert. "The Road Not Taken." *Mountain Interval.* New York: Henry Holt, 1920.

Hawking, Stephen, and Leonard Mlodinow. *The Grand Design.* New York: Bantam Books, 2010.

James, William. "The Dilemma of Determinism." *The Will to Believe and Other Essays.* New York: Dover, 1979.

———. *A Pluralistic Universe* in *William James: Writings 1902–1910.* Ed. Bruce Kuklick. New York: Library of America, 1987.

———. *The Principles of Psychology.* Cambridge, MA: Harvard UP, 1938.

Kane, Robert. "New Directions for an Ancient Problem." In *Free Will.* Ed. Robert Kane. Malden, MA: Blackwell, 2002.

Milton, John. *Complete Poems and Major Prose.* Ed. Merritt Y. Hughes. New York: Odyssey Press, 1957.

Robinson, Luther Emerson. *Abraham Lincoln as Man of Letters.* Chicago: Reilly and Britton, 1918.

Sartre, Jean-Paul. *Being and Nothingness: An Essay in Phenomenological Ontology.* Trans. Hazel E. Barnes. New York: Philosophical Library, 1957.

Tec, Nechama. "Helping Behavior and Rescue During the Holocaust." In *Lessons and Legacies: The Meaning of the Holocaust in a Changing World*, eds. Peter Hayes. Evanston: Northwestern UP, 1991.

Vedral, Vlatko. "Living in a Quantum World." *Scientific American* 304.6 (June 2011): 38–47.

Wolf, Susan. "Sanity and the Metaphysics of Responsibility." In *Free Will.* Ed. Robert Kane. Malden, MA: Blackwell, 2002.

Wrestling with the God(s)

Benjamin W. Westervelt
Lewis & Clark College

One of the six required "texts" in Lewis & Clark College's Core program is three books of the Bible: *Genesis*, *Exodus*, and *Matthew*. Even such a slender biblical requirement, however, can pose some notable challenges for the Core instructor when confronted by the anxious student who asks: "what does it mean?" My text for illuminating the challenges and opportunities the Bible presents to first year students is the *pericope* in Genesis sometimes called "Jacob Wrestles with the Angel," Gen. 32, verses 22 through 32, inclusive (all Bible quotations hereafter are from the Revised Standard Version, unless otherwise stated). My thesis is that the jarring gallimaufry of interpretations that students encounter as they explore the interpretive traditions that have accumulated around this text in fact opens them up to a way of reading and thinking about texts that is new, unfamiliar, exciting...and necessary.

The scene: Jacob has been sojourning with his mother's clan in Haran for the past twenty years, ever since fleeing his home after cheating his twin brother, Esau, first out of his birthright and then out of the blessing intended for him by their father, Isaac. At Gen. 32. 22–32, Jacob is on the verge of crossing back into Canaan with his two wives, his concubines, and his children; a much feared meeting with his murderously angry twin (Gen. 27.41) looms. Jacob sends his family over the border–which is the river Jabbok–but waits alone (on one bank or the other–it is unclear), at night (Barthes 86). There at the ford of the Jabbok he encounters "a man" with whom he wrestles through the night until the break of day. The mysterious "man" is unable to defeat Jacob, even after resorting to injuring Jacob's hip. As dawn threatens, the "man" begs Jacob to let him go, but Jacob refuses until the man blesses him. The man asks Jacob's name, and when he learns it is *Jacob*–literally, "the heel clutcher" (Bloom and Rosenberg 97)—he gives Jacob a new name, *Israel*—literally "the struggler with God" (or "God clutcher," the etymology that Harold Bloom favors): "because you have held on among gods unnamed as well as men, and you have overcome" (97, 114). Jacob (still—so much for the name change!) asks **his** name, which the man refuses to give. He does, however, bless him. Then Jacob names the place where he wrestled with the man *Peniel*, "for I have seen God face to face, and my life is preserved." As the sun rises, he limps past Penuel and into Canaan for his meeting with Esau. The technical explanation for the change from *Peniel* to *Penuel* need not detain us here. The passage ends with the observation that to this day, the children of Israel do not eat the "muscle that shrank" where the man touched it. A wonderfully strange, familiar, and packed text.

What on earth does it mean? The student and the instructor are well entitled to ask! Two ways of answering the question are: first, what are some of the classic Jewish and Christian interpretations of this story? And second, what sense have modern scholars made of it? As it happens, the sets of explanations are not only different: they are incompatible. One way to make sense of these differences is to realize (and more importantly, to demonstrate to students) that modern scholars try to work out what the passage means; the traditions—Jewish and Christian, literary, artistic, dramatic and musical–have the additional function of helping to illuminate what something **else** means too. Another way one might put the distinction is modern biblical scholars try to get at what the biblical texts mean; students in core courses also need to immerse themselves in what such texts have meant.

First the classic traditions. The Jewish *midrash* tradition–from the Hebrew word for "investigate" or "interpret"—offers a rich banquet of interpretations. The first, which is itself canonical and (as it happens) precedes the true midrashic era, may be found in the book of the prophet Hosea (c. 725). The prophet adverts to the "Jacobskampf," as modern German biblical scholars call it: "in his strength he [Jacob] struggled with God. Yes, he struggled with the Angel and prevailed; he wept, and sought favor from Him" (Hosea 12. 3b–4). The author of Hosea has significantly cleaned up the story, homogenizing conflicting elements of it and drawing a moral lesson. It is God's Angel with whom Jacob wrestled and against whom he prevailed; and we are further told that Jacob wept and sought God's favor.

The housekeeping activities of Hosea reflect the emergence of an influential reading of this passage. The mysterious stranger is God (or God's designated agent), and the struggle at the ford of the Jabbok is a test. I stress that neither aspect of this interpretation is obviously supported by Gen. 32 itself, a subject of interest to students, since it seems to show Genesis in conflict with Hosea. Variations on this interpretation, however, will have a long and productive history.

Josephus (37–100 C.E), in his *Jewish Antiquities*, a sort of *Reader's Digest* version of the Hebrew Bible, follows this line. After Jacob has defeated the "spectre," it reveals itself to him, asserting that he should not "imagine that it was a puny adversary whom he had mastered: he had defeated an angel of God and should deem this victory an omen of great blessings to come" (Josephus 159).

Rashi or Rabbi Solomon Ben Isaac (1040–1105) pulls on this thread further. The Angel was perhaps the "Guardian angel of Esau" and wanted to get away at dawn in order to "say praises at day." What Rashi has done, in other words, is to contextualize the pericope by exploring other aspects of canonical scripture. Following Hosea but changing the subject of "wept," Rashi asserts that the **angel** wept and made supplication to him (Jacob) and informed him that God would bless him at Bethel (Ben Isaiah et al. 330–333).

The *Zohar* (13th century C.E.)–literally "radiance"—one of the central texts of the Jewish mystical tradition called *Kabala*—introduces a different interpretation and a different interpretive strategy, one that cannot be made compatible with the traditions we have just been examining. There, rather than contextualize the story, the *Zohar's* rabbinical protagonists allegorize it. Jacob's struggle is at night (the time of the moon, the "defective light"), when the soul leaves the body, and it is uniquely vulnerable to possession by "impure female spirits" (Zohar 1:169b, 26) who inhabit "ruins, unyielding fields, desolate wilderness" (1:170a, 27). The Rabbis draw a moral conclusion from our story:

> One must thoroughly protect himself from them [the impure female spirits], following paths of Torah, not defiling himself with them. For everyone who sleeps in bed at night tastes a taste of death, his soul departing from him. Since body is left without holy soul, impure spirit who is poised, spreads upon him and he is defiled. . . . Come and see: Even though Jacob was beloved by the blessed Holy One, because he remained alone, an alien spirit poised to couple with him. (Zohar 1:169b–170a. 26–27)

In his magisterial *Legends of the Bible*, Louis Ginzberg compiles into one redaction the further elaborations of this story. Although it seems to be all of a piece, the notes in Ginzberg's final volume untangle the complex redactive strands of the "final" version of the story. The stranger at the ford of the Jabbok is now a shepherd who tricks Jacob into helping him move the stranger's own animals across the river. When the angry Jacob seizes the stranger to thrash him for his deception (Jacob the arch deceiver here deceived), he is revealed to be the archangel Michael, who decides to "let him [Jacob] know once for all with whom he has had dealings" (Ginzberg 186). Michael is on the verge of injuring Jacob when God appears to rebuke Michael for causing a "blemish in my priest Jacob" (Ginzberg 186). The Angel Raphael is summoned to heal Jacob. There follows a wonderfully novelized elaboration that features the other Angels calling, "Ascend, O Michael, the time of song hath come, and if thou art not in heaven to lead the choir, none will sing." Ginzberg continues: "Michael entreated Jacob with supplications to let him go [thank you Hosea!], for he feared the 'Angels of Arabot' would consume him with fire, if he were not there to start the songs of praise at the proper time" (Ginzberg 186). Jacob refuses to let him go, however, until he blesses him, which he eventually and reluctantly does. Clearly we have come a long way from the stark narrative of the canonical pericope itself.

The trend toward interpreting by allegorizing also became the dominant way to make sense of this text among Christian readers and commentators too. Ambrose (c. 337/40–397 C.E.), who played a critical role in bringing to the Latin West the allegorizing interpretive methods of Alexandria, used the pericope as a metaphor for the righteous person's struggle to attain virtue: "What is it to wrestle with God other than to enter upon the struggle for virtue, to contend with one who is stronger and to become a better imitator of God than the others are?" (Sheridan 219). His younger contemporary, Augustine (354–430 C.E.), took a different tack. In *The City of God* and Sermon 229, he discerned Jesus and the Jews prefigured in the pericope: "When Jacob returned from Mesopotamia with his children, an angel wrestled with him, representing Christ; and while he wrestled, though the angel surpassed Jacob in strength, he still seemed to succumb to him, and Jacob to prevail. In the same sort of way, the Lord Christ too succumbed to the Jews, they prevailed when they killed him" (Sheridan 219). In Sermon 5, on the other hand, Augustine finds in Jacob's "withered thigh" a type for bad Christians: "He [Jacob] is blessed with respect to those who live good lives; he limps with respect to those who live bad lives. But each kind is still included in one man" (Sheridan 220).

Thus already by the Middle Ages, Jewish and Christian commentators alike had systematized a biblical hermeneutic that recognized different senses (as few as two or as many as ten) whereby meaning could be found in every word of the Bible. Augustine famously articulated these different senses of scripture in his treatise, *On Christian Teaching*; Nicholas of Lyra's late thirteenth-century doggerel captures one version of this four-fold system: "Littera gesta docet/quid credas allegoria/quid agas tropologia/quo tendas anagogia" ("The letter teaches events/allegory what you should believe/tropology what you should do/anagogy where you should aim") (Ocker 265).

Jewish exegetes developed a remarkably similar interpretive palette, known as *Pardes. Pardes* means "orchard," as in an "orchard of meaning"; but it is also "an acronym for *peshat*, exegesis based on context; *remez*, philosophical or typological exegesis; *derash*, rabbinic homiletical and legal midrashim; and *sod*, mystical interpretation. Whiles this is not identical to the four-fold system found in Christian interpretation . . . the parallels are clear" (Hauser and Watson 18–19). With this method, both Christian and Jewish could find the most extravagant meanings in the most unlikely of places, as long as the interpretation did not conflict with other parts of the text and tradition.

This open-endedness about making meaning with a passage such as this is particularly noteworthy in artistic representations, two of which I offer here. The first, by Rembrandt, is entitled "Jacob wrestles with the Angel" and was probably painted around 1659/60; it shows Jacob and the angel locked in an intimate even sensual embrace (Fig. 1). The angel has a leg cocked around the small of Jacob's back and seems to be holding Jacob tightly to its breast. The pose certainly suggests sexual intimacy and traces a fine line between violence and sexuality; the ambiguity of the physical contact is captured in the ambiguous expression on the angel's face. The other image is very different. Painted in 1878 by Gustave Moreau, it shows Jacob struggling with all his might against an angel who is easily holding him off with one hand and has an unmistakable look of boredom on its divine face—if it had a free hand it would perhaps be inspecting the angelic fingernails (Fig. 2)! The former features a numinous antagonist; it illuminates a carnal and immanent representation of the relationship between the divine and the human. The latter image, on the other hand, suggests divine distance and transcendence with human impotence. The ambiguous expression of Rembrandt's angel and the bored expression of Moreau's angel illustrate vividly the polyvalency of this text. Neither image is possible, however, without the penumbra of interpretations that now accompany the culturally embedded text, and neither is "wrong," notwithstanding the very different conclusions they prompt.

Fig. 1. Rembrandt Harmensz van Rijn. "Jacob Wrestles with the Angel" (1659/60). oil on canvas, Gemäldegalerie der Staatlichen Museen. Berlin.

Similar productive ambiguity pervades Tony Kushner's explicit treatment of the story in his award-winning play, *Angels in America.* The image of wrestling with the Angel and what it means is central to the play and looms large in its climax, where an interpretation of it is literally acted out. But it is an ancillary reference that best captures the productive ambiguity of the story. There, Joe, the closeted and conflicted Mormon, recounts to his wife an experience from his childhood:

> I had a book of Bible stories when I was a kid. There was a picture I'd look at twenty times every day: Jacob wrestles with the angel. I don't really remember the story, or why the wrestling—just the picture. Jacob is young and very strong. The angel is . . . a beautiful man, with golden hair and wings, of course. I still dream about it. Many nights. I'm . . . It's me. In that struggle. Fierce, and unfair. The angel is not human, and it holds nothing back, so how could anyone human win, what kind of a fight is that? It's not just. Losing means your soul thrown down in the dust, your heart torn out from God's. But you can't not lose. (Kushner 49–50)

Kushner ingeniously selects different parts of the tradition–for example, the sexual ambiguity suggested by Rembrandt's painting and the contest between human and divine that are such a central theme of the medieval Christian and Jewish traditions– to make new meaning about the pain of denying one's sexual identity and the inexorable assertion of that identity.

By way of contrast, a rather different approach comes closest to answering the question, "what does it mean?" and suggests how it would be a disaster for first-year students in the Core to begin (and I fear end) with it. Claus Westermann reviews and critiques the fruits of modern literary and form criticism as applied to Gen. 32. 22–32. The heart of the story, he asserts, is a very old local folktale about battling with the

Fig. 2. Gustave Moreau, "Jacob and the Angel" (1878), watercolor on canvas, Musée Gustave, Paris.

river spirit that seeks to impede passage across the Jabbok. The Yahwist or J author of the Pentateuch took the story and inserted it into his account of Jacob's itinerary home from Haran. Inserted it, one might add, with considerable literary sophistication. Subsequent redactors—probably the Priestly or P author—much later added further material, especially the name change (Jacob to Israel) and the etiology of the taboo on eating meat from the thigh. Westermann flatly denies the identification of the "man" with God or the Angel: "All the profound theological consequences drawn from Jacob's supposed encounter with God. . . . Have no basis in the text" (519). The numinous spirit is neither God nor an Angel but rather a night-bound, evil spirit whom Jacob vanquishes. The blessing that he demands and receives is the transfer of some of the demon's power to Jacob, and the demon sensibly refuses to share its name lest it lose even more power. The Yahwist inserts the story to provide additional structure for the itinerary of Jacob's return to Canaan. "The whole return journey in chapters 32–33 is determined by encounters. Here Jacob encounters a lethal danger in the attack of the river demon. Jacob survives, even though limping, and carries from it a power, the 'blessing' of the superhuman opponent. 'And the sun rose on him' when he continued; he has experienced that God was with him. He can now go on to meet his brother" (Westermann 521).

    Westermann and scholars of his ilk probably come closest to answering our plaintive undergraduate question. It is a grave mistake, however, to give such an answer to the inquiring *first-year* student. On the contrary, I would ask them to begin with Kushner's *midrash* in *Angels in America* or a similar contemporary interpretation and then stalk the story back to Genesis. In the Core, one should do everything possible to encourage students **not** to seek a definitive (and exclusive) answer, but rather to go down the interpretive rabbit hole of the traditions, following Rashi and Rabbi El'azar, Ambrose and Augustine, Rembrandt and Moreau: there they will find wonders to explore, to admire, and to use. And knowing the story in its kaleidoscopic variations, they will begin to recognize it all over the canons of Western art and literature. Beyond that blessing, they will begin to see that all of these interpretive trajectories, Westermann and fellow historical-critical scholars, Kushner and Josephus, are all working within relating trajectories. Patristic and medieval Christian exegetes devised their interpretations explicitly to refute contemporary Jewish interpretations; Ginzberg assembled his unitary Jewish myth cycle in response the needs of liberal reform Jewish communities, especially in the United States at the beginning of the twentieth century; and, imbued with post-enlightenment secular ideals, practioners of the historical-critical method devised an exegesis that did not require theological assumptions at all in order to be explanatory. These different interpretations may have been intended to be incompatible, but they are also locked in a permanent embrace—one might almost say they wrestle with each other. When students get to the point where they can transcend, or at least see their way to transcending, the several exclusivist claims of these trajectories, they will be on the threshold of some significant insights about how readers operate and how texts endure.

In the spirit of "Go ye and do likewise!" I offer an allegorical application of my text. Jacob is the first semester student, who crosses into Canaan or College (Caanan College?) via the Jabbok or the Core course we visit upon our first-year students. We make them read difficult texts—they struggle through the night sometimes, reading them, thinking about them, writing about them (though hopefully not through the night before the paper is due). Yet when dawn comes they have their blessing to go with their limp. They now know how at least to begin to read and to think and write about such complex texts.

What is more, what applies to students applies as well to the recalcitrant faculty who protest their inadequacy to teach "outside their field." On the contrary, such learned amateurs are indispensable to the success of Core programs that rely on broad-based faculty participation. Their brief to illuminate Core texts is not that anyone can come up with a fanciful interpretation or reading. Rather, it is the example of the quest to make sense and to make connections—to cast lines from tradition to tradition—that such faculty can offer. Far from putting up with the amateur bungling of such guides, Core programs need such guides because they are precisely the faculty members who can model for students the kind of generous, disciplined, and open-ended inquiry that we claim the liberal arts inculcates.

Works Cited

Armstrong, Karen. *The Bible: A Biography*. New York: Atlantic Monthly, 2007.

Ben Isaiah, Abraham, et al., eds. *The Pentateuch and Rashi's Commentary: A Linear Translation into English*. Vol. 1. Brooklyn: S,S & R, 1976.

Bloom, Harold, and David Rosenberg. *The Book of J*. Trans. David Rosenberg. New York: Grove Hill, 1990.

Ginzberg, Louis. *Legends of the Bible*. Vol. 1. New York: Simon and Schuster, 1956.

Hauser, Alan J. and Duane F. Watson, eds. *The Medieval through the Reformation Periods*. Vol. 2. Grand Rapids, MI: Eerdmans, 2009.

Josephus. *Jewish Antiquities*. Trans. H. st. J. Thackeray. Vol. 4. Cambridge: Harvard UP, 1978.

Kushner, Tony. *Angels in America: A Gay Fantasia on National Themes*. New York: Theatre Communications Group, 1993.

Moreau, Gustave. *Jacob and the Angel*. 1878. Watercolor on canvas. Musée Gustave Moreau, Paris. 7 June 2010. <http://cgfa.acropolisinc.com/moreau/p-moreau16.htm>

Ocker, Christopher. "Scholastic Interpretation of the Bible." Eds. Alan J. Hauser and Duane F. Watson. Vol. 2. Grand Rapids, MI: Eerdmans, 2009.

Rembrandt Harmensz van Rijn. *Jacob Wrestles with the Angel*. 1659/60. Oil on canvas. Gemäldegalerie der Staatlichen Museen, Berlin. 7 June 2010. <http://www.uni leipzig.de/ru/bilder/ erzvaet/b4-49.jpg>

Sheridan, Mark, ed. *Genesis 12–50. Ancient Christian Commentary on Scripture: Old Testament*. Vol. 2. Downers Grove, IL: InterVarsity, 2002.

Westermann, Claus. *Genesis 12–36: A Continental Commentary*. Trans. John J. Scullion. Minneapolis: Fortress, 1995.

The Zohar: Pritzker Edition. Vol. 3. Trans. Daniel C. Matt. Stanford: Stanford UP, 2006.

Teaching Frederick Douglass as a Master Rhetorician

Hollis Robbins
The Johns Hopkins University

Teaching Frederick Douglass's *Narrative of the Life of Frederick Douglass* (1845) as a core text poses particular challenges when taught alongside texts for which the condition and circumstances of the author are not under scrutiny. It is all too easy to teach Douglass's *Narrative* as a simple chronicle of a life–an honest and straight-forward account of one man's escape from slavery to freedom. But this approach privileges the author over the text, unsettling the whole point of teaching core texts (or a Great Book, in the case of my own experience teaching the *Narrative*). And yet the issue of authorship is an integral part of the publication of Douglass's *Narrative*, which features prefatory material by white abolitionists William Lloyd Garrison and Wendell Phillips testifying that the author is who he says he is: a fugitive slave literate enough to tell his own story. Is it possible or advisable to teach Douglass's *Narrative* as a literary performance first and an authentic account second? What would be gained and what would be lost?

Frederick Douglass was promoted by his supporters as a "representative Negro in America," though he was hardly representative in remarkable facility with language. He was a far more exacting master of words than his supporters and readers. For a fugitive slave he was perhaps too literate. From master rhetoricians in the pages of *The Columbian Orator*, Douglass learned the arts of verbal performance and persuasion. He understood that his language must capture his readers as well as convince them of his truthfulness. He would be a master of words; his readers and listeners would be in thrall to his power.

But how could Douglass be both slave and master at once? This is the central

problematic of Douglass's text. He needed to speak from two positions simultaneously: as an uneducated slave and as an educated gentleman who understood the
complex attitudes of his audience: curious, prurient, skeptical, horrified, and admir-
ing. He needed to tailor his story to sound like perfect truth. So his topic was not
slavery in general but a particular slave: himself. Douglass created a voice that could
talk about himself at a critical distance from himself. He emphasized his early habits
of self-reflection and desire for education; this voice, or character—his younger, enslaved self—tells the story of himself in the language of the older, free, and educated
self. Garrison writes, "Mr. Douglass has very properly chosen to write ... in his own
style and according to the best of his ability, rather than to employ someone else."
Douglass's "style" is a calculated performance.

Douglass begins the *Narrative* almost brazenly by addressing his readers' interest in sexual assault under slavery, revealing his origins as the child of a slave mother
and an unknown white father—perhaps his master. I ask students to highlight the first
sentence of the first five paragraphs:

1. I was born in Tuckahoe, near Hillsborough, and about twelve miles
    from Easton, in Talbot County, Maryland.

2. My mother was named Harriet Bailey.

3. My father was a white man.

4. I never saw my mother, to know her as such, more than four or five
    times in my life; and each of these times was very short in duration, and
    at night.

5. Called thus suddenly away, she left me without the slightest intimation
    of who my father was.

These five simple sentences establish Douglass as an honest and straightforward
narrator, a man interested in accuracy ("twelve miles," "four or five times"), whose
language is far from unsophisticated ("slightest intimation"). The task of highlight-
ing the first sentence of each paragraph instills the habit of attending to paragraph
structure generally.

We then count the sentences in the first paragraph. There are twelve:

I was born in Tuckahoe, near Hillsborough, and about twelve miles from Easton, in
Talbot County, Maryland. I have no accurate knowledge of my age, never having
seen any authentic record containing it. By far the larger part of the slaves know as
little of their ages as horses know of theirs, and it is the wish of most masters within
my knowledge to keep their slaves thus ignorant. I do not remember to have ever
met a slave who could tell of his birthday. They seldom come nearer to it than plant-
ing-time, harvest-time, cherry-time, spring-time, or fall-time. A want of information
concerning my own was a source of unhappiness to me even during childhood. The
white children could tell their ages. I could not tell why I ought to be deprived of the
same privilege. I was not allowed to make any inquiries of my master concerning it.
He deemed all such inquiries on the part of a slave improper and impertinent, and
evidence of a restless spirit. The nearest estimate I can give makes me now between

twenty-seven and twenty-eight years of age. I come to this, from hearing my master say, some time during 1835, I was about seventeen years old.

We read each one out loud. I ask my students: who is speaking? The uneducated slave or the educated gentleman? A conversation generally follows in which students begin by observing that an uneducated person would not use terms like "thus," "seldom," and "evidence of a restless spirit." But, others reply, only a person who experienced these things first hand would know of them. Yet how would a young, uneducated Douglass have described these things at the time? Could he only have understood the import of his experience from his position as an adult? Does his telling it in a language he didn't have at the time make the story any less truthful? What, then is the relationship of the language of adulthood and the experience of childhood generally?

None of these questions emerge from a focus on "authenticity" or from asking why Douglass begins his *Narrative* where he does.

We move to the third paragraph, in which the difference between the language of adulthood and the experience of childhood is far more obvious:

> My father was a white man. He was admitted to be such by all I ever heard speak of my parentage. The opinion was also whispered that my master was my father; but of the correctness of this opinion, I know nothing; the means of knowing was withheld from me. My mother and I were separated when I was but an infant—before I knew her as my mother. It is a common custom, in the part of Maryland from which I ran away, to part children from their mothers at a very early age.

The paragraph ratifies the students' understanding that there is always a rhetorical distance between the event and the telling of the event. All narratives are performances, even "authentic" or "truthful" ones.

Anti-slavery writers before and after the publishing of Douglass's *Narrative* worried about how to write about slavery in ways that were realistic and uplifting and provocative—but provocative in the right way. Literary scholars have argued that scenes of whipping, sexual violence, and cruelty in narratives of slavery were often more arousing to readers than intended, a kind of "pious pornography" whose appeal was masked by its overt claims of a positive social agenda. An explicit portrait of sexual predation risks the danger of turning the reader's attention from more inspirational themes. Understanding these dangers sheds light on Douglass's astonishing rhetorical maneuvers in the first chapter of his *Narrative* as he moves from the implicit assault on his mother to an appalling scene of sexual violence he witnesses first hand:

> I have often been awakened at the dawn of day by the most heart-rending shrieks of an own aunt of mine, whom he used to tie up to a joist, and whip upon her naked back till she was literally covered with blood. . . .

> I remember the first time I ever witnessed this horrible exhibition. I was quite a child, but I well remember it. I never shall forget it whilst I remember any thing.

> Why master was so careful of her, may be safely left to conjecture. She was a woman of noble form, and of graceful proportions, having very few equals, and fewer superiors, in personal appearance, among the colored or white women of our neighborhood.

> Had he been a man of pure morals himself, he might have been thought interested in protecting the innocence of my aunt: but those who knew him will not suspect him of any such virtue. Before he commenced whipping Aunt Hester, he took her into the kitchen, and stripped her from neck to waist, leaving her neck, shoulders, and back, entirely naked. . . .
>
> He then told her to cross her hands, calling her at the same time a d–d b–h. After crossing her hands, he tied them with a strong rope, and led her to a stool under a large hook in the joist, put in for the purpose. He made her get upon the stool, and tied her hands to the hook. She now stood fair for his infernal purpose. Her arms were stretched up at their full length, so that she stood upon the ends of her toes.

I ask the students: what does he not say, but which is obvious? After horrified giggles they begin to list what is unsaid. Douglass does not say that the master was sleeping with Aunt Hester. He does not say that the master was getting pleasure from whipping her. He does not mention her naked breasts. But all these things are unmistakable. Just as Douglass knows that the reader will fill in the blanks of "d–d b–h," he knows that his readers will fill in other blanks. This is a performance of an astute narrator gauging the tastes of his audience in order to describe a scene of sexual violence. Douglass refrains from saying anything personally demeaning about his Aunt Hester even as he makes the reader see how shameful the scene was. Douglass tells the story in two voices: the slave who witnessed it and the educated gentleman who is reporting it to his presumably equally gentle (albeit curious) readers.

Does Douglass's masterful rhetoric undermine his veracity? Do we doubt the truthfulness of the story because of the manner of the telling? No, students usually say. If it were more explicit it would be demeaning to his Aunt Hester, and it would be pornographic. If it were less explicit it would be boring. As it is, it provokes outrage alone.

Thus the first chapter of Douglass's narrative begins and ends with stories of sex between white men and slave women, even while the narrator has established himself as a gentleman. Douglass's rhetorical project is evident: he will tell a narrative in which he is the only "real" man in his experience, by which he means, the only gentleman. Every other man in his narrative falls short. In Chapter IV, for example, Douglass describes the overseer Mr. Gore:

> He was just proud enough to demand the most debasing homage of the slave, and quite servile enough to crouch, himself, at the feet of the master. He was ambitious enough to be contented with nothing short of the highest rank of overseers, and persevering enough to reach the height of his ambition. . . . His presence was painful; his eye flashed confusion; and seldom was his sharp, shrill voice heard, without producing horror and trembling in their ranks.

Douglass deftly deploys the words "crouch," "confusion," and "shrill" in his description of the ambitious overseer. Mr. Gore, these words suggest, is not a real man.

By contrast Douglass, in Chapter V, refers to his own servile condition in a manly and respectful way. Consider these descriptions:

> I was kept almost naked—no shoes, no stockings, no jacket, no trousers, nothing on but a coarse tow linen shirt.

> My feet have been so cracked with the frost that the pen with which I am writing might be laid in the gashes.

> The children were then called. like so many pigs. and like so many pigs they would come and devour the mush.

While he describes himself as being kept "almost naked," the image of stockings, jacket, and trousers remind the reader what Douglass is now clothed in. While his feet were once cracked with frost, the reader is reminded that the same Douglass is now holding a pen. The slave children who devour mush like pigs are collected under the pronoun "they," not "we." Douglass will not present himself in anything but a respectful light.

Douglass's description of his fistfight with Covey in Chapter X provides an opportunity for a close-reading assignment to identify rhetorical maneuvers that keep the narrator at a critical distance, maintaining Douglass's dignity. The narrator shifts imperceptibly between the defiantly combative slave and the calm, educated man. "You have seen how a man was made a slave; you shall see how a slave was made a man," the narrator proclaims, using a chiasmus to emphasize Douglass's rising and Covey's falling. Covey is described as a "snake," who operates "secretly," "by surprise," and with "cunning." In the fight, Douglass "seized Covey hard by the throat," while Covey "trembled like a leaf." There must have been moments where Covey had the upper hand, as Douglass recounts "[w]e were at it for nearly two hours." But, as the older Douglass declares, "[t]he battle with Mr. Covey was the turning point in my career as a slave. It rekindled the few expiring embers of freedom, and revived within me a sense of my own manhood. It recalled the departed self-confidence." Focusing on word choice and voice rather than the story told, students better understand the power of Douglass's rhetorical mastery.

Finally, I distribute the table of contents from the *Columbian Orator*, which includes Cato's speech before the Roman Senate, William Pitt's speeches in Parliament, Sheridan's speeches before Parliament, George Washington's "Address to the People of the United States," works by Socrates, Milton, and Addison. I hand out Pitt's speech on the Stamp Act, 1766 (nine sentences):

> Gentlemen. Sir. I have been charged with giving birth to sedition in America. They have spoken their sentiments with freedom against this unhappy act, and that freedom has become their crime. Sorry I am to hear the liberty of speech in this house. imputed as a crime. No gentleman ought to be afraid to exercise it. It is a liberty by which the gentleman who calumniates it might have profited, and by which he ought to have profited. He ought to have desisted from this project. The gentleman tells us, America is obstinate; America is almost in open rebellion. I rejoice that America has resisted. Three million of people so dead to all feelings of liberty, as voluntarily to submit to be slaves, would have been fit instruments to make slaves of the rest.

Students easily see the model for Douglass's "style." As Douglass describes in the 1855 version of his *Narrative*, "The reading of these speeches added much to my limited stock of language, and enabled me to give tongue to many interesting thoughts, which had frequently flashed through my soul, and died away for want of utterance." In short, Douglass learned to write from the words of others; the words of other provided the tools to tell his own story. From great men Douglass learned to master language. to make language *his* slave. This is the story of the *Narrative*.

Teaching Arendt's *Eichmann in Jerusalem* as an Introduction to Philosophy

Joshua A. Shmikler
Boston College

It may seem strange for me to recommend Arendt's *Eichmann in Jerusalem* as an excellent text to introduce philosophy to American undergraduates. Hannah Arendt rejected the title of "philosopher" most of her career and, in a 1964 television interview, even announced: "I do not belong to the circle of philosophers. My profession, if one can speak of it at all, is political theory. . . . I have said goodbye to philosophy once and for all" ("WR?" 3). Additionally, Arendt's *Eichmann in Jerusalem* provoked an intense controversy. Her unconventional interpretation of the "banality" of S.S. Lieutenant-Colonel Adolf Eichmann, the Chief of the Jewish Office of the Gestapo who played a key role in implementing the Nazi extermination of European Jewry, angered many and even led to the dissolution of several of her friendships. "Why," one might ask, "should I introduce philosophy with a controversial book by someone who claimed not to be a philosopher?"

In response, I would suggest that Arendt never followed through with her hyperbolic proposal to "say goodbye to philosophy once and for all." Arendt was educated in philosophy, and all of her works bear the mark of her philosophical concerns. Over the course of her career, Arendt's writings became increasingly focused upon the mental activities of human beings, and, as Elizabeth Young-Bruehl notes, by 1972 Arendt "had given up her reluctance to call herself a philosopher rather than a political theorist" (327). Arendt's concern with the *vita contemplativa* culminates in the uncompleted *The Life of the Mind* (1978), her most explicitly philosophical work. Arendt explains that her "venture from the relatively safe fields of political science and theory into these rather awesome matters" (matters of philosophical concern) stemmed primarily from her attendance at the trial of Adolf Eichmann (*LM* Vol.1.3). To simplify the matter somewhat: it was Arendt's recognition of Eichmann's "absence of thinking" which led her to take an increased interest in philosophy proper (*LM* Vol.1.4). As such, it is not unreasonable to assume that reading Arendt's *Eichmann in Jerusalem* might have a similar effect and excite philosophical interest in American students.

Furthermore, I believe that the storm of controversy surrounding Arendt's *Eichmann in Jerusalem* in no way detracts from its educational value. The hostile debates, which immediately followed Arendt's series of articles on the Eichmann trial and continued long after her publication of *Eichmann in Jerusalem*, reflect the way that Arendt's work challenged traditional conceptions of the Holocaust, totalitarianism, normality, civil disobedience, success, evil, justice, and responsibility. Arendt's unusual understanding of the character of Adolf Eichmann, her nuanced assessment of various types of collaboration with the Nazis and her analysis of the legitimacy of the trial in Jerusalem were often misunderstood by her most virulent critics. While I do believe that Arendt's *Eichmann in Jerusalem* may be legitimately criticized for its harsh tone, as well as for its occasional lack of sympathy and discretion, I agree with Seyla Benhabib's claim that Arendt's work "is to be credited for being among the first to encourage facing the facts of the Nazi regime and the Holocaust in all their naked horror" (71). It is Arendt's attempt to force her readers to grapple with these facts, occasionally by means of sarcasm, irony, and black humor, that makes her work both controversial and of serious educational import.

The chief reasons I have for recommending Arendt's *Eichmann in Jerusalem*, however, are not associated with the trajectory of Arendt's intellectual interests or with the reception of her writing. Instead, I maintain that Arendt's *Eichmann in Jerusalem* is an excellent text with which to introduce philosophy to American undergraduates because it effectively engages the world that students inhabit. Specifically, many of my pupils have difficulty understanding why they should care about philosophical thought and do not realize that they hold unexamined opinions. It is because Arendt's *Eichmann in Jerusalem* may be used to address both of these challenges that I believe it serves as an outstanding introduction to philosophy.

Most of the American undergraduates I have taught initially express a bias against philosophical thought. These students assume that philosophy is a wholly "abstract" discipline, one that has no connection to the manner in which a person lives his life. Students vocalize this prejudice in claims such as "philosophy has no practical usefulness" and "it does not matter what people think about or say; it only matters what they do." Obviously, if this anti-intellectualism remains unchallenged, then students will be unable to benefit from philosophical education. For a teacher cannot reasonably expect students to devote their time and energy to something they believe to be worthless.

Due to American undergraduates' tendency to devalue philosophical thinking, Arendt's *Eichmann in Jerusalem* is an extraordinarily beneficial text. Not only does the work reveal the intimate connection that exists between thinking and acting, but it also paints a frightening picture of the unexamined life. This is accomplished by means of Arendt's analysis of Eichmann's most serious character flaw.

At several key points in *Eichmann in Jerusalem*, Arendt discusses the flaws she sees in Eichmann's character. Although she highlights Eichmann's poor memory and tendency to boast, Arendt ultimately maintains that Eichmann's most decisive flaw was "his almost total inability to look at anything from the other fellow's point of view" (*EJ* 47–48). Arendt explains that this lack of moral imagination was the result of Eichmann's failure to speak or to think for himself. Instead of engaging in genuine communication with others, Eichmann employed a battery of stock phrases and self-invented clichés, which allowed him to shield himself from the presence of others and feel "elated." Instead of stopping and thinking about the legitimacy of the Third Reich and its policies, Eichmann refused to face reality by unquestioningly subordinating himself to the commands of Hitler, the laws of the Nazi regime, and the morally bankrupt opinions of prominent Germans. Arendt provides several specific examples of such thoughtlessness, including Eichmann's belief that he was doing justice to the Jews of Austria by expelling them from the country, Eichmann's horrifying suggestion that he had a "normal, human encounter" with Kommerzialrat Storfer in Auschwitz, and Eichmann's outrageous assumption that an Israeli prison guard would sympathize with his failure to attain the rank of Colonel in the S.S. (*EJ* 51). Arendt reveals that it was Eichmann's unwillingness to think seriously about what he was doing that led him "to ship millions of men, women, and children to their death with great zeal and meticulous care," to participate in genocide without believing that he was doing wrong (*EJ* 25).

In encouraging students to investigate the connection between Eichmann's refusal to think and his willingness to perform evil actions because they were deemed socially acceptable, Arendt's text challenges students to reevaluate their unexamined prejudice against philosophical thought. *Eichmann in Jerusalem* accomplishes this by compelling students to consider the potentially monstrous consequences of the thoughtless obedience to social norms, engendered by an utter lack of philosophical reflection. Arendt's disquieting account of Eichmann's most decisive character flaw, which she claims is in no way identical to a lack of native intelligence, highlights the importance of taking individual responsibility for one's own thoughts, words, and deeds. In this way, Arendt's text encourages students to become more open to the study and practice of philosophy.

Along with their bias against philosophy, many American undergraduates I have encountered are initially unwilling to think deeply about their own opinions or subject their views to the considered judgments of others. Instead, students vocally advocate a soft form of relativism, which manifests itself in claims such as "I do not need to defend my opinion because it is true for me" and "one should never judge other people." Such views make a genuine understanding of and appreciation for philosophy difficult. This is because philosophy makes sense only if serious thought about one's self and others might help a person to improve his life. However, there is one area where a majority of my students feel confident discussing their judgments. When asked for examples of evil, students immediately mention the Nazis, explaining that the Nazis were evil because their ideological commitments led them to "kill many people." The primary lesson students draw from the Holocaust, which they have learned from repeatedly studying it in history class, is that one should not hold racist or anti-Semitic beliefs.

In light of American undergraduates' confidence in their understanding of what caused the actions of the Nazis, Arendt's *Eichmann in Jerusalem* is an extremely useful text. Not only does the work focus on a topic students believe they know something about and are willing to earnestly discuss, but it also leads them to re-examine and broaden their simplified understanding of what led the Nazis to perpetrate the Holocaust. This is accomplished by Arendt's careful analysis of *why* Eichmann became "a willing instrument in the [Nazi] organization of mass murder" (*EJ* 279).

The first eight chapters of *Eichmann in Jerusalem* contain unsettling discussions of Eichmann's motivations, considering and undermining the view that all Nazi murderers were motivated by racist and anti-Semitic ideology. For Arendt reveals that Eichmann did not join the Nazis for ideological reasons, that he was unfamiliar with the Party program, and that he never read *Mein Kampf*. Moreover, Arendt notes that Eichmann had a Jewish mistress in Vienna, intervened to save the lives of his Jewish relatives, protested against the desecrators of Herzl's grave, said he "never harbored any ill feelings against his victims and...never made a secret of that fact" and exhibited no signs of mental or moral derangement when examined by psychologists (*EJ* 30). Instead of a frenzied anti-Semite or racist, Arendt reveals Eichmann to be "a joiner," less concerned with the beliefs of the group to which he belonged than with the opportunity to join "a movement" and achieve career success. Arendt convincingly argues that it was Eichmann's immoderate admiration for Hitler's rise, his unwavering obedience to the law (regardless of its source), his willingness to silence his conscience when it did not mirror the standards of "good society" and his refusal to think, to speak, or to act for himself which led Eichmann to become a "desk murderer."

In encouraging students to think more about the causes of Nazi evil, to consider whether the actions of most Nazis resulted from ideological fanaticism or from the thoughtless abdication of personal responsibility, Arendt's text helps students to examine one of their previously unquestioned opinions. In this way, *Eichmann in Jerusalem* facilitates thought and self-examination among students, inspiring pupils to become more open to the investigation of both their own opinions and the opinions of others. Arendt's unconventional account of Eichmann, whose character she claims most people at the trial misunderstood, demonstrates to students that philosophical reflection has the power to reveal truths about a situation, truths which remain inaccessible should one's opinions remain unexamined.

Hannah Arendt's *Eichmann in Jerusalem* offers an account of evil that leads students to rethink their anti-intellectual biases and forces them to question their unexamined opinions about the Holocaust. It is for these reasons that I believe it is an excellent work with which to introduce philosophy. Arendt's text succeeds because it gives students a reason to care about philosophical thought and acquaints students with some of the insights made possible by philosophical reflection. By effectively engaging the world that students inhabit, Arendt's *Eichmann in Jerusalem* allows American undergraduates to make a genuine beginning in philosophy; for as Margaret Canovan rightly claims: "Hannah Arendt is preeminently the theorist of beginnings" (vii).

Works Cited

Arendt, Hannah. *Eichmann in Jerusalem: A Report on the Banality of Evil.* New York: Penguin Books, 2006.

———. *The Life of the Mind.* San Diego: Harcourt, 1978.

———. "What Remains? The Language Remains: 'A Conversation with Günter Gaus.'" Trans. Joan Stambaugh. *The Portable Hannah Arendt.* Ed. Peter Baehr. New York: Penguin Books, 2000. 3–22.

Benhabib, Seyla. "Arendt's Eichmann in Jerusalem." *The Cambridge Companion to Hannah Arendt.* Ed. Dana Villa. Cambridge: Cambridge UP, 2000. 65–85.

Canovan, Margaret. "Introduction." *The Human Condition.* Chicago: U of Chicago P, 1998. vii–xx.

Young-Bruehl, Elisabeth. *Hannah Arendt: For Love of the World.* New Haven: Yale UP, 1982.

Using Fiction and Nonfiction by Barbara Kingsolver to Help Students Think Across Disciplines

Heather McGovern
The Richard Stockton College of New Jersey

At The Richard Stockton College of New Jersey, the one experience *all* students share, whether they start at the college, or, like half of our students, transfer in, is that they take a course in General Integration and Synthesis (GIS). Our official description of a GIS course in our *Undergrad Bulletin* notes that these courses

> constitute the capstone of the General Studies curriculum [and] are designed to assist students already acquainted with the various modes of knowledge to understand their connections. GIS courses seek to help the student transcend specialization and gain perspective on self, areas of knowledge, and the human condition. GIS courses are not just interdisciplinary but transcend the limits of any one of the existing academic divisions at Stockton either in subject matter or content or by directly addressing those human experiences—individual and social—that transcend the boundaries within academic life. GIS courses are focused on questions of enduring value.

One of the courses I teach, GIS Voices and Visions on the Environment, is a course in environmental rhetoric. My course description reads as follows: "In this course, we will explore one concept, *environment*, through the rhetoric of six types of texts: art, nonfiction writing, film, fiction writing, science writing, and music. Through those six units, we'll explore primary examples, discuss historical and cultural changes in attitude, and analyze ethical perspectives. In addition to exploring what "environment" has meant to artists, writers, and musicians, we'll discuss the possibilities inherent to different genres: what can paintings offer that photographs cannot, and vice versa? How is the environment portrayed differently in science writing than in writing aimed toward a more generalized audience or produced for a different purpose? What can film do that a novel cannot, and vice versa? How is music similar to and different from poetry, in its possibilities and/or its potential reach in current American culture?"

The course goals include the following:

- Students should be more aware of environmental discourse at work in their own lives.

- Students should better recognize, understand, critique, and respond to others' perspectives on the environment.

- Students, through reading, viewing, and listening to environmental rhetoric in a variety of genres from a variety of disciplines, should understand the environment and perspectives on it in a holistic, interdisciplinary manner.

- Students should better understand and be able to more effectively communicate their own perspectives on the environment.

Given the goals and nature of the course, I do not use a textbook in this class, as I have not been able to find a textbook that we would use a large enough portion of to warrant the expense. Instead, I bring artwork and music and film into the class and assign short stories, poems, essays, and scientific articles. In addition, I always require students to read one nonfiction book; so far, for a variety of reasons, that book has always been *Silent Spring*. In addition, students always read one novel that has environmental rhetoric embedded within it. The last few times I've taught the course, we've read Barbara Kingsolver's *Prodigal Summer*. Many students tell me this is one of the first books they've actually read in their adult lives, or they are impressed with their ability to finish such a long book. The book is good as literature for undergraduate students—it is reasonably easy to understand upon a first, casual reading, but each time I read it I see new complexities and connections. One of the things I've come to like best about how it works in my class, however, is how it juxtaposes with a nonfiction essay, also by Barbara Kingsolver, called "Setting Free the Crabs." Both pieces address some of the same environmental issues; they teach some of the same scientific lessons. But because they belong to different genres, they do this very differently. The nonfiction essay focuses on our treatment of other species, especially endangered species, through the lens of selfish and unselfish love. It argues that when we try to save one individual—to bring a rare orchid to our home garden or an endangered tropical bird to our house—we are damaging the species, because that individual cannot reproduce. This is, Kingsolver argues, a selfish love. A less selfish love might value a keystone predator or microbe as much as a panda, or mourn the loss of all the orchids. The essay also presents an argument about how a biblical mandate to "have dominion over the fish of the sea, the fowl of the air, and every thing that creepeth upon the earth" puts many humans in our culture in a position of power and self-interest that makes it harder to be unselfish ("Setting Free" 65). Kingsolver notes that we want to "preserve the wilds, sure, but we still want to own them somehow, and take home a snapshot as proof" ("Setting Free" 66).

Some of my students find the nonfiction essay more compelling. Of course, at fourteen pages, more of them read all of it, and it is simpler to read and understand. Many of them note that the author saying her husband is an ornithologist ("Setting Free" 68) gives her credibility in the nonfiction essay. In the essay, she is able to use logos and ethos more effectively, to craft a careful argument. She tells of the damage done in Hawaii by the introduced species, domesticated pig ("Setting Free" 70). She explains that when we use pesticides to kill mosquitoes, we also damage butterflies, birds, lizards, and critical zooplankton ("Setting Free" 73). She makes herself human, noting that she still kills mosquitoes that are biting her, and admits "it's taking me some time to get to that emotional plane where I can love a mosquito" ("Setting Free" 73).

The novel, *Prodigal Summer*, which is 444 pages long, addresses some of the same environmental issues. Instead of the author speaking as herself, we receive multiple perspectives on life and environmental issues through the views of different characters. One character, Deanna, who is a scientist, seems perhaps most like the Kingsolver we saw in the essay, and from Deanna we get lessons about the need to protect endangered species, the importance of predators in the ecosystem, and the dangers of introduced species. Another couple of characters swap interpretations of the biblical mandate to have dominion over the creatures of the earth and argue over the benefits and dangers of pesticides. While in the nonfiction essay, her argument about the effects of religion is brief and one-sided, because the novel is longer, Kingsolver can spend more time on it and present multiple perspectives on it—and this is true for many environmental issues raised in the novel. However, Kingsolver also cannot speak with the same authority in the novel, a piece of fiction, as she can in the essay. In addition, some novel readers may overlook the environmental arguments altogether to focus on the human story. Others may pay more attention to the environmental arguments—or be exposed to them at all—because they are drawn to the human story.

A deeper comparison of how each work treats one issue may help give you, my audience today, a sense of the comparisons my students are able to make. In the nonfiction essay, Kingsolver quotes statistics about the number of songbirds killed by domesticated cats, saying "Scientists who study this destruction have estimated, for example, that domesticated cats in North America kill as many as four million songbirds *every day*. The millions of feral cats out there—those that have left human habitation and are fed by no one but themselves—add many more deaths to this toll" ("Setting Free" 72). Kingsolver offers this example as support for the topic sentences in a paragraph: "The trick here is to distinguish between caring about the good of a species and caring about an individual creature. These two things can actually run at cross purposes" ("Setting Free" 72). In the novel, the character Deanna, who can be (and perhaps is) more radical threatens that "If a feral cat wandered up here from some farm and started wrecking nests and killing birds and having babies in the woods? I'd trap it and drown it in the creek" (*Prodigal Summer* 177). Even in the novel, another character then argues with Deanna, who ultimately says she isn't sure what she'd do, but repeats the argument that Kingsolver made in the nonfiction essay: "I don't love animals as *individuals*. I guess that's the way to put it," she said." I love them as whole species. I feel like they should have the right to persist in their own ways. If there's a house cat put here by human carelessness, I can remedy that by taking one life, or ignore it and let the mistake go on and on" (*Prodigal Summer* 177).

By making characters the mouthpieces for environmental messages, Kingsolver complicates the messages. We see that one character is meant to represent a traditional approach to farming and other species, and that another is meant to represent a more organic approach—initially, we're introduced to these two characters as both representing fairly extreme, radical perspectives on opposite ends of the continuum, but we also learn of one's life work trying to rescue the American Chestnut and see a kind of love blossom between the two. In the novel, more than in the essay, we realize that environmental messages in our lives are often communicated by the real, complex humans with whom we disagree and whom we respect; we want to shake our heads at what they say, but we also want to hug them.

In my class, we read these pieces in different course units, but assigning both means that class discussion and student writing can help students explore genre—in this case, the rhetorical advantages and disadvantages of nonfiction and fiction. Students think about class concepts like audience, purpose, pathos, ethos, and logos in a new light as they realize that the author makes similar arguments in different ways and/or to different effect. They debate about which genre is more effective—and inevitably some students favor one reading over the other—and this helps them understand how each of us is different, and what will (or won't) persuade us differs, too.

These texts, then, demand of students what the class is supposed to demand: that they integrate and synthesize, that they see connections across disciplines and the value in different ways of thinking and knowing, and that they deal with important issues that affect us and the world in which we live.

Works Cited

Kingsolver, Barbara. *Prodigal Summer*. New York: Harper Collins Publisher, 2000.
———. "Setting Free the Crabs." In *Small Wonder*, New York: Harper Collins, 2002: 60–74.
The Richard Stockton College of New Jersey. *Undergrad Bulletin 2008–2010*. 2008. March 2010. <http://intraweb.stockton.edu/eyos/bulletinpdf/content/docs/oldbulletins/Undergraduate_Bulletin_2008-2010.pdf>.

Part II. When Cultures Meet

Montesquieu's *Persian Letters* and the Uses of Comparativism

Henry C. Clark
Clemson University

I came to this conference looking for insights into how one teaches a cultural-literacy curriculum of classic texts to students whose attention spans and reading habits are not what ours were when we began our careers. No text and no curriculum is perfect, but the work I have chosen to discuss today has a certain number of real advantages. Montesquieu's *Persian Letters* is not only one of the first important works of the European Enlightenment; it also is a work that paradoxically has a special significance for American readers. I say paradoxically because in form and literary art, it is a work thoroughly European, I might even say thoroughly French, in spirit. Filled with esoteric references and elusive maneuvers appropriate to a literary community that was already in the 1720s engaged in its century-long game of cat and mouse with the royal censors, the work swims in the waters of irony and indirection that would come to define the Enlightenment aesthetic.

But it is also a thoroughly "American" work because it is a work centrally, and in some sense exclusively, about liberty. Donald Lutz once showed that Montesquieu was far and away the most frequently cited author in America between 1760 and 1800, garnering over four times as many citations as the runner-up candidate in the quotations sweepstakes, John Locke (Lutz). That was primarily because of the pervasive influence of his later work *The Spirit of the Laws* (1748), with its exposition of the constitutional requirements of liberty, especially in Book Eleven, Chapter Six where the concepts of the separation of powers and of the supposed checks and balances of the English political system are canonically described.

But in *Persian Letters*, we get a treatment of liberty that is perhaps more complex, more difficult to unravel, more psychological than constitutional in nature, and yet in many ways more presentable to this generation of college students than the one contained in his later and more familiar masterpiece. Whereas constitutional questions often seem dry and settled to our current students, the presentation of liberty as a cultural problem is alive and entirely contemporary in the earlier work. This is so for at least three important reasons.

First, the problem of liberty is presented primarily through the experiences of women. I have sometimes been amazed at the skill and insight with which students are able to distinguish the various female characters in the seraglio and chart their specific relationships and their differing fates and trajectories. The character of Roxana in particular, who becomes the chief vehicle through whom the theme of natural liberty is conveyed, is a riveting example of the phenomenon of speaking truth to power that is deeply embedded in Christian and classical culture, but that strikes us in new ways by virtue of being presented to us in a female voice. The contrast between the arrogant, pompous and ultimately self-deluding master Usbek and his beloved, virtuous, but ultimately rebellious wife Roxana becomes a resonant dramatization of the natural liberty that would be such a central theme of Enlightenment political and social thought.

Second, by putting the story on a cross-cultural canvas, Montesquieu makes it speak to this generation of students. He uses contemporary depictions of the Islamic world as a mirror with which to show his own Frenchmen some uncomfortable truths about their own civilization. My experience is that students not only notice that the author is attributing un-free institutions to non-Western peoples, but that the scintillating stories and ringing speeches in defense of liberty are also made mostly by the Persian characters.

Third, the method of exposition is one that comports well with the learning styles of this generation of students, and this in two ways. The overarching adventure is pushed along with the help of a number of discrete stories, presented either as answers to philosophical questions or as the products of fortuitous discovery—of letters, for example. Young people are increasingly familiar with game theory, and Montesquieu's own mind gravitated toward the thought experiment. The story of the Troglodytes in letters 11–14, for example, is presented as the answer by Usbek to a question by his friend Mirza about the nature of justice. It provides a very agreeable method of introducing students to the broad outlines of Shaftesbury's critique of Hobbes's moral psychology, a critique that Montesquieu also made throughout his career (Shaftesbury 68–9).

Another reason why the method of exposition works is because Montesquieu's dating of the letters makes of the story a kind of puzzle, which a generation raised on CSI and the rest of the Bruckheimer franchise enjoys the challenge of unraveling. For example, in letter 141, Rica tells Usbek a story within a story about an Arab woman who gets her revenge against a ruthless husband by sending one of her celestial partners down to earth to smash his unjust household rule. When the students realize that this letter was sent to Usbek after the disastrous suicide of his favorite new wife Roxana, which is told at the very end of the work, it throws a whole new light for them on the unfolding of the larger story, and it makes them attentive to the

Pinter-like narrative strategies used by Montesquieu throughout.

Teaching Montesquieu is a little like slicing the ice cores in Greenland. Every place you dig in, it seems that a random sample of the whole history of the species confronts you. For example, letters 112–22 begin with Rhedi's question to Usbek whether population is rising or declining, but as they unfold, the letters unfold an elaborate and multilayered series of sociological and historical comparisons. There is the comparison between ancient and modern, which was a structuring heuristic device throughout Montesquieu's career. But there is also a comparison between the pagan Romans, on the one hand, and the Christians and Muslims (ranged on the same side), on the other. Then, there is a comparison between commercial and non-commercial peoples in the modern world, and also a comparison between Catholic and Protestant states within the state-system of contemporary Europe. Students get a little dizzy during this analytical merry-go-round, but when it becomes clear to them that each one of these comparisons is a spoke that protrudes from the same thematic hub of liberty, which in turn is related to the other discussions of liberty throughout the work, they see the larger architecture of the work take shape before their eyes, and this makes for an unusually agreeable introduction to the age of reason, and to one of the true classics of world literature.

Works Cited

Lutz, Donald S. "The Relative Influence of European Writers on Late Eighteenth-Century American Political Thought." *American Political Science Review* 78 (1984): 189–97.

Shaftesbury, Anthony. "Of Wit and Humour." *Characteristicks of Men, Manners, Opinions, Times.* Ed. Douglas Den Uyl. Indianapolis: Liberty Fund, 2001.

Ishmael's Initiation into the Revelry of Work

Emily Heyne
University of Dallas

The world of American whaling is dead. It has been forever relegated to the museums of New England harbors and to PBS documentaries. No student, I venture to say, will return from a semester at sea to boast of having harpooned a whale. Whaling is the industry of a bygone era and now viewed as our shameful sin against Nature. Nevertheless, it has undergone a resurrection, and while posing no danger to the great leviathan, the whaling world still lives on and produces plentiful oil and light in the imaginations of all who read Melville's *Moby Dick.* Chapter by chapter, Melville recreates life on a whaleship, and for the past century, Americans have readily climbed aboard. What fuels our attraction to this watery world, and why do we continually insist that our students join the ranks of whalemen alongside Ishmael? Perhaps the reason is that we still share Ishmael's world—a world, as Melville shows, dominated by the likes of Peleg and Bildad.

Though they appear in only three short, humorous scenes in the whole of *Moby Dick,* Peleg and Bildad are integral figures in Ishmael's world. Let us examine their final appearance in the novel, the setting sail of the *Pequod,* in order to illustrate this point.

The day is Christmas, "a short, cold Christmas," Ishmael tells us. Aunt Charity has most charitably fitted the *Pequod* with all the supplies, comforts, and hymnals necessary for a three year voyage. The crew has come aboard, the tent on deck is collapsed, and the ship is ready to up anchor and away. With Captain Ahab still concealed in his quarters below deck, the journey of the fated whale ship thus gets underway with its two Quaker owners piloting it out of port.

At one end of the ship, pious Bildad, brother to that good Aunt Charity, watches over the bows for the anchor while he sings a "dismal stave of psalmody" (Melville 94). Bildad speaks with a diction straight from the King James Bible, and he had earlier justified paying Ishmael low wages by appealing to St. Matthew's Gospel. Now, as he heads the first watch, Bildad sings of the Promised Land:

> Sweet fields beyond the swelling flood.
> Stand dressed in living green.
> So to the Jews old Canaan stood.
> While Jordan rolled between. (95)

In contrast to Bildad (who had requested that no profane songs be sung on board), Captain Peleg oversees the crew at the other end of the ship and "rip[s] and sw[ears] in the most frightful manner" with commands of " 'Muster 'em aft here—blast 'em!'" and " 'Aft here, ye sons of bachelors'" (93, 94). Meanwhile, Ishmael, disconcerted by Peleg's fitful capering and cursing commands, pauses for a moment at his work on his handspike as he considers the "perils [he] ran, in starting on the voyage with such a devil of a pilot" (95). Nevertheless, he comforts himself with the thought that, "in pious Bildad might be found some salvation," and he relishes the words of Bildad's song: "Never did those sweet words sound more sweetly to me than then. They were full of hope and fruition" (95).

Ishmael's musings on piety, salvation, and eternal summers, however, are abruptly halted when he is kicked in the rear by Captain Peleg. " 'Is that the way they heave in the marchant service?' [Peleg] roar[s]. 'Spring, thou sheep-head; spring, and break thy backbone!'" (95). Ishmael is thus brought back to task, and shortly thereafter the two piloting owners take reluctant and permanent leave of their ship, leaving it in the charge of Captain Ahab.

Though the imperturbable Bildad and the cantankerous Peleg could not be further apart in their management styles; nevertheless, they are singular in their aim, that is, the success of the *Pequod's* endeavor. They both hope to see their ship return in three years' time fully laden with barrels of oil. Furthermore, the two owners are practically identical in regards to their Quaker upbringings, their previous careers as whalemen, and their Nantucket residence. What is more, the extreme differences in their personalities and contrasting approaches to work may belie an underlying similarity. That is, they both uphold a rigorous work ethic; it is said of Bildad that though he never swore at his men during his sea-going days, he "somehow got an inordinate quality of cruel, unmitigated hard work out of them.... Indolence and idleness perished before him" (72). A mere look from Bildad would have a sailor scrambling for work. Peleg's sailors, in turn, are literally kick-started into a fury of action. Both captains, therefore, regard industry as a virtue and motivate their laborers by a fear of violence: Peleg's by the fear of immediate violence to their ears and backsides, and Bildad's by a sort of fear of violence in the hereafter, for they seem to feel the coming judgment of the Almighty in his scowl.

In these two owners, Melville gives us a picture of the American culture in which Ishmael lives—and the one from which he continually tries to escape. It is the America that was made prosperous through diligence, discipline, and devotion—the

America we still recognize and pride ourselves in today. Whether driven by greed or God, we're the nation that gets things done. Bildad and Peleg would not be so comical were they not so familiar to us. The hard-nosed Bildad we still find admirable. "His own person," Ishmael says of him, "was the exact embodiment of his utilitarian character. On his long, gaunt body, he carried no spare flesh, no superfluous beard" (72). The severity and rigor of the two captains are as much of America's heritage as Ben Franklin's frugality, but Ishmael seems rather reluctant to adopt it as his own.

In fact, when explaining his motivation to ship as a common sailor, he readily admits, "I abominate all honorable respectable toils, trials, tribulations of every kind whatsoever. It is all I can do to take care of myself, without taking care of ships, barques, brigs, schooners, and whatnot" (14). Though he certainly recognizes he'll have to put in his fair share of work as a whaleman and be ordered about a bit, his true motivations for shipping aboard involve everything but the actual work of whaling. He takes to the sea for its romance, for its fresh air and mystical vibrations: in short, for the wonders of the watery world he believes will inspire great reveries and deep meditations. Recall that in the opening pages, Ishmael admits to having suicidal tendencies, and he believes his cure for these sullen moods is to take to the sea. But what he hopes to gain from his ocean voyage is not a true resurrection back to an active life, but a more complete escape from it. For instance, he relishes his time atop the mast head, where instead of singing out for sighted whales, he experiences a sort of death, an escape from all the "carking cares of earth," without having to undergo the bodily pains of dying (139).

> The mast-head . . . to a dreamy meditative man...is delightful. . . . There you stand, lost in the infinite series of the sea, with nothing ruffled but the waves. The tranced ship indolently rolls, the drowsy trade winds blow; everything revolves you into languor. For the most part, in this tropic whaling life, a sublime uneventfulness invests you; you hear no news; read no gazettes; extras with startling accounts of commonplaces never delude you into unnecessary excitements; you hear of no domestic afflictions; bankrupt securities; fall of stocks; are never troubled with the thought of what you shall have for dinner—for all your meals for three years and more are snugly stowed in casks. (137)

Ishmael says that the sea is his "substitute for pistol and ball" (12). But let us be clear: standing one hundred feet above the sea is his true substitute; seamanship certainly is not.

So what is a captain to do with a sunken-eyed sailor like Ishmael? Bildad's and Peleg's methods of intimidation and violence have little effect on this dreamer. After being briefly horrified by Peleg's kick, he dismisses it, thinking, "Captain Peleg must have been drinking something today" (95). And, rather than being inspired to work by Bildad's pious psalmody on the Promised Land, Ishmael relishes the sweet words as a mental respite from the cold and understands them to mean that many a "pleasant haven" may be in store for him yet (95). The Quaker culture that regards bodily toil and productivity as a mark of holiness seems to be the very culture Ishmael deplores. As narrator, Ishmael presents Bildad and Peleg as comic caricatures, yet he greatly admires Bulkington, a sailor whom he believes to be a deep, earnest thinker. Melville here seems to suggest that the American work ethic, the belief in hard work now, heaven later, may in fact breed a generation of brooding Ishmaels, of Platonists who seek escape from the body and attempt to cultivate immediate eternal repose in their heads. Ishmael even surmises that the whale-fisheries have become an "asylum for many romantic, melancholy, and absent-minded men" (139). A detachment from all things bodily and an inability to understand the role of the physical within the spiritual or philosophical realms, as Melville shows, pervade the world of *Moby Dick*.

Yet what follows from our narrator are not pages of indefinite ocean reveries, but beginning mid-way through the book, Ishmael supplies a detailed, voluminous account of the physical work of whaling—the process of capturing, hauling in, cutting, boiling, and stowing the whale—and an unprecedented investigation into the body of the whale—its head, tail, skin, bones, blubber, and brains. What effects this change in him? What has Melville proposed here as the cure for the dichotomy of slavishness and escapism in the American work culture? Put simply, it is an encounter with a whale.

Almost half-way through the novel, after the crew has sworn to give chase to Moby Dick and after they have unsuccessfully lowered for a whale in an oncoming gale, the first whale is finally killed in Chapter Sixty-One. It is here that Ishmael's transformation takes place. The scene begins as Ishmael keeps watch on the fore-mast-head. He says, "I idly swayed in what seemed an enchanted air. No resolution could withstand it; in that dreamy mood losing all consciousness, at last my soul went out of my body" (241). For a moment, he achieves the disembodied state, that is, death, for which he had so longed. But then, he says, "Some invisible, gracious agent preserved me; with a shock I came back to life. And lo! Close under our lee, not forty fathoms off, a gigantic Sperm Whale lay rolling in the water" (242). The ship becomes a flurry of action and exclamations, and this time, the hunt is successful. Stubb kills the whale.

Here, the narrative makes a distinctive shift. Ishmael describes his organization of subsequent chapters as akin to the organic growth of branches and twigs from a tree trunk (246). Just as Ishmael "comes back to life" with this whale encounter, his narrative too takes on a life of its own. In the next forty five chapters, we hear very little of Ahab or his quest for the white whale. Instead of interpretations of the whale as represented in art or in scientific manuscripts—as Ishmael had supplied in the first half of the book—he now gives us firsthand accounts of his experience with the whale's body. He relishes the chance to see, smell, feel, and taste its flesh and blubber. He spends pages hypothesizing about the nature of its spout, its field of vision, and the markings on its skin. Whereas he once desired to live only in his mind in order to understand the mysteries of the universe, he now delves into a rich, sensory experience in order to understand the mysteries of the whale.

Moreover, Ishmael approaches the descriptions of whaling in a tone of rapturous excitement and joy, certainly not that of burdensome drudgery. Though whaling is undoubtedly hard, dangerous, and violent work, Ishmael rejoices in it. Consider the way he describes the process of stripping the blubber: "And thus the work proceeds; the two tackles hoisting and lowering simultaneously; both whale and windlass heaving, the heavers singing, the blubber-room gentlemen coiling, the mates scarfing, the ship straining, and all hands swearing" (259). The work of whaling is a symphony of coordinated effort. While thus engaged in the labor, Ishmael comes to believe that "attainable felicity" is not to be found "in the intellect or fancy" (349). Rather, he discovers true felicity in the sweet task of squeezing spermaceti from hardened lumps back into fluid. "I am ready to squeeze case eternally," he exclaims, and imagines angels in heaven doing likewise (349). A glimpse of paradise is to be had here, in the physical, working world.

Perhaps we can then begin to see the significance of the *Pequod*'s Christmas day departure. The voyage of the *Pequod* is, for Ishmael, an initiation into the blessings of bodily, incarnated world. The mysteries of the universe, Ishmael discovers, can be contemplated by great attention, not to abstract ideas, but to both the living and dead body of the whale and by mindfulness to his own physical interaction with it. At one point he claims he has "been blessed with an opportunity to dissect [the whale] in miniature" (373). By examining the whale's body, he comes to appreciate his own, exclaiming, "I rejoice in my spine," for a spine upholds a "full and noble soul" (294). A man's character, he says, can be discerned by his backbone. This is the same Ishmael who, pre-*Pequod*, had boasted, "Methinks me body is but the lees of my better being. In fact, take my body who will, take it, I say, it is not me" (41). Through his study of the whale's body, Ishmael is made whole: he discerns a unity between body and soul, between thought and labor.

Ahab's journey, by contrast, is a relentless rejection of the good of the body. In fact, in Ahab's first soliloquy in the novel, he discards his pipe, refusing to be comforted by it any longer. After the loss of his leg, he cannot reconcile his own suffering with a world that still allows physical pleasure. Even on that last and fateful day of the chase, he resents the cumbersome body as an impediment to thought. Much like the mast-head Platonist, he asserts, "Thinking is, or ought to be, a coolness and a calmness; and our poor hearts throb, and our poor brains beat too much for that" (460). Thus, as a fitting end to his indignant quest, the whale line wraps around his neck and—we can assume—beheads him.

From Ishmael's encounter with the whale, then, students may learn to work and read aright. They may learn to triumph over the culture wrought by Peleg and Bildad, not through escapism, but through real engagement in the task before them. Moreover, they may learn to choose with greater discernment their own professions and future texts. Ishmael, for instance, no longer reads those daily gazettes and extras which had earlier so bogged him down. Nor do I think he would find the words of Bildad's psalmody on the Promised Land quite so sweet as he did upon the outset of his voyage. The whale's body is now his text, and in that, he finds great significance. Furthermore, he now dialogues regularly with other whalemen and reads naturalistic, mythological, and religious accounts of the whale and its history. His physical labor of hunting, cutting, and boiling the body of the whale supplies physical light for the landsmen back home; yet, it will also supply that intellectual light for his own meditations and those of his future readers. As educators, our task must be to confront our students with the mysteries of the whale. After all, we are educating not just future thinkers, but future workers, and those two terms, as Ishmael has shown us, need not be in opposition.

Works Cited

Melville, Herman. *Moby Dick*. Eds. Harrison Hayford and Hershel Parker. New York: W.W. Norton, 1967.

Engaging Cultures: Is the Melting Pot Still Cooking?

Lyndall Nairn
Lynchburg College

The theme of this year's ACTC conference, "engaging cultures," is exemplified in the circumstances of immigrants: people who move from one country to another cannot help but encounter different worldviews as they come in contact with unfamiliar cultures. Today's media and websites abound with discussions about immigrants. On the negative side, we hear strident criticisms of immigrants living in the US illegally: they take jobs from deserving Americans; they abuse the welfare system; they don't pay for medical services; and they expect their kids to be educated for free while the parents supposedly pay no taxes. Furthermore, any foreign terrorists on our shores present the threat of violence and even death to innocent American citizens. On the positive side, most Americans consider that "the melting pot" of immigrants from many nations who formed American society in the eighteenth and nineteenth centuries has provided a fundamental strength for our culture today, and most Americans feel proud of their tradition of generosity to newcomers as illustrated by the words of Lazarus's poem on the Statue of Liberty:

> Give me your tired, your poor,
> Your huddled masses yearning to breathe free,
> The wretched refuse of your teeming shore,
> Send these, the homeless, tempest-tossed to me,
> I lift my lamp beside the golden door! (Lazarus 399)

One core text that can help students weigh the merits of the two sides of the immigrants' debate is *My Antonia* by Willa Cather. This novel provides students with the safe buffer of a fictional story set over a hundred years ago so that they can consider both the problems and advantages presented by immigrants from a relatively objective point of view. The next step in this discussion involves considering our own American identity today: to what extent can we benefit from learning to appreciate elements of foreign cultures instead of merely viewing immigrants as "Others" who are alien and different from us?

Cather sets *My Antonia* up as an autobiography of Jim Burden, an orphan, who leaves Virginia at age ten to go to live with his grandparents, who are farmers on the Nebraska prairie near the small town of Black Hawk. People of many different backgrounds have recently settled in this rural community: Scandinavians, Russians, Bohemians (like the young Antonia Shimerda, the novel's namesake) and people who consider themselves Americans, like the Burdens. In this ethnically mixed environment, Cather is quite fair in the way she presents the negative view of immigrants in late-nineteenth-century America in that some of the immigrants do not fulfill their societal responsibilities and that some of the American characters are unreasonably narrow-minded and even prejudiced in their attitudes to foreigners. For example, Jake Marpole, the farmhand who accompanies the ten-year-old Jim Burden on his train trip from Virginia to Nebraska, warns Jim, "You [are] likely to get diseases from foreigners" (Cather 6). Later in the Black Hawk school, when Jim speaks up for the newly arrived immigrants, some of whom he knows are much better educated and more cultured than anyone else in Black Hawk, Jim's school mates "look at [him] blankly . . . [because they thought that] all foreigners were ignorant people who couldn't speak English" (Cather 98). In fact, the behavior of a few of the immigrants does reinforce this negative stereotype. Specifically, Antonia's parents, the Shimerdas, arrive in Nebraska totally unprepared for the farming life. They lack not only the skills and the resources for farming but also the necessary determination to learn how to survive in this difficult environment, as seen by Mr. Shimerda's suicide during his first Nebraska winter (Cather 52). However, Mrs. Shimerda is the one who presents the most unattractive view of immigrants. When Jim's grandparents help the Shimerdas through the winter with gifts, food, and advice (like "buy hens"), instead of thanking them, Mrs. Shimerda just berates them with accusations that if she had as much as they have, she would be able to cook and care for her family much better than Mrs. Burden looks after her family (Cather 37, 44). Mrs. Shimerda speaks in such an "envious, complaining tone" that Jim can only conclude that "she was a conceited, boastful old thing, and even misfortune could not humble her" (Cather 45). Furthermore, Cather includes examples of immigrants exploiting and mistreating each other, such as Krajiek, a fellow Bohemian, who overcharges the Shimerdas for their land and who seems to have played a suspicious role in Mr. Shimerda's death (39, 56). In all these ways, Cather is realistic about the problems of the immigrants' experience on the American frontier.

Nevertheless, Cather's overall attitude towards immigrants remains positive and optimistic. Despite all the difficulties of their first years on the prairie, the Shimerdas and the other immigrant farming families survive and eventually flourish because of their hard work. Their determination to get ahead pays off by the time the second generation is in their thirties mainly because the teenage girls are willing to do domestic work and the boys, hard labor, unlike their more class-conscious American counterparts, whose parents do not want to send their children into service (Cather 98). As a result of this hard work by the first and second generations, the immigrant families are able to pay off their debs more quickly than the other farmers who keep their daughters at home and their sons in school for longer.

By the time the Bohemian and Scandinavian girls are in their late teens and early twenties, Jim is enthralled by their joy of life: they work hard and play hard, loving to dance, laugh, and tell stories. Jim admires the spirit of these hired girls who have come to live and work in town, and he is contemptuous of the town boys who are attracted to the vivacious country girls but who are not brave enough to broach the social norms that prohibit these American boys from becoming familiar with the girls whose cultural, religious, and language backgrounds are different from their own; Jim says of these town boys: "The respect for respectability was stronger than any desire in Black Hawk youth" (Cather 98). In contrast, Jim is less inhibited by class consciousness and perceives the immigrant girls only positively and even romantically, saying, "If there were no girls like them in the world, there would be no poetry" (Cather 129).

How can we explain Jim's attitude, which is markedly more tolerant and open-minded than that of his peers? Some of Jim's approach can be explained by the influence of his grandparents. At the time of Mr. Shimerda's death, Jim's grandmother was indignant when the Norwegians refused to allow Mr. Shimerda to be buried in their cemetery because he had committed suicide; she says, "If these foreigners are so clannish, . . . we'll have to have an American graveyard that will be more liberal-minded" (Cather 56). Jim is impressed when at Mr. Shimerda's funeral, his grandfather "prayed that if any man there had been remiss toward the stranger come to a far country, God would forgive him and soften his heart" (Cather 58). Jim's grandparents provide a role model of acceptance, which is reinforced by Jim's firsthand experience with the immigrant families in and around Black Hawk. Later in life, Jim tells Antonia's children that he once loved their mother; moreover, he had been so much in love with Lena Lingard that he found it difficult to leave Nebraska to go away to study (Cather 164, 139). Despite the shortcomings of some of these immigrants and the judgmental attitudes of many of his American peers, Jim is able to appreciate the positive aspects of the immigrants' experience and the character strengths of the immigrants themselves.

In this way, Jim Burden presents an example of someone who has overcome Edward Said's hurdle of the "Other." Said explains that we create this problem when we categorize people according to their values, which are either familiar or different from our own; Said maintains that it is both dangerous and dehumanizing to view the Self positively and the Other negatively (325, 332). Part of Jim Burden's appeal as a character is that he moves beyond the comfortable either/or thinking of "us versus them" and manages to overcome the natural human weakness of regarding familiar values and customs in a more favorable light than those that are unfamiliar. In this way, Cather has presented Jim Burden and the immigrant families of Black Hawk as an example of the American melting pot as a work in progress. With hard work and joy of life on the part of the immigrants and with an accepting attitude on the part of Jim and his grandparents, the integration experience can become a success, and an admirable American identity can be formed.

In the last sentence of *My Antonia*, Jim reveals his deep appreciation of his shared upbringing with Antonia and the other young people of the immigrant families in Nebraska; that rich experience with "Others" different from him formed his character and shaped his identity in significantly positive ways; Jim concludes the novel: "Whatever we had missed, we possessed the precious, the incommunicable past" (Cather 175). Jim's reflection echoes the framing narrator's comments about Jim's nature in the introduction to the novel: "No disappointments have been severe enough to chill his naturally romantic and ardent disposition. This disposition . . . has been one of the strongest elements in his success" (Cather 2). The narrator admires Jim's pragmatism, determination, enthusiasm, sympathetic interest in others, and love of the Western outdoors experience (Cather 2). All these positive traits in the American character, which in Jim's case developed under the influence of his generous grandparents and his hard-working, cheerful immigrant friends and neighbors, come shining through in *My Antonia*. Willa Cather's novel presents a challenge to today's students to keep on developing a positive American identity by appreciating the strengths and values of newly arrived immigrants. We can all benefit by keeping the melting pot cooking.

Works Cited

Cather, Willa. *My Antonia*. New York: Dover, 1994.

Lazarus, Emma. "The New Colossus." *Shaping Truth: Culture, Expression, and Creativity: Lynchburg College Symposium Readings*. Vol. III. Ed. Barbara Rothermel. 3rd ed. Philadelphia: Xlibris, 2005.

Said, Edward. *Orientalism*. New York: Vintage, 1979.

The Problem with Engaging Worlds: E. M. Forster's Suspicion of Culture

Tim Mackin
Saint Michael's College

E. M. Forster's *A Passage to India* is, to borrow a phrase from one of his contemporaries, a voyage out, an Englishman's encounter with the non-European world. Engaging worlds and cultures is thus the explicit subject of Forster's novel, which makes *A Passage to India* of particular interest to our conference. For all its focus on the meeting of English and Indian culture, however, *A Passage to India* takes a generally negative view of the kind of categorical thinking that underlies cultural and political identities, and thus the whole idea of engaging worlds. In Forster's view, engaging worlds is an obstacle rather than a goal, a way of closing off the world rather than entering into it.

Forster's suspicion of the political and cultural spheres has not been lost on academic readers of the novel, who often see this tendency as evidence of a persistent Orientalism. Edward Said speaks for a number of critics when he claims that *A Passage to India* "founders on the undodgeable effects of Indian nationalism" (203). The problem, according to Said, is that Forster ultimately validates the colonial enterprise by ignoring the political realities of his subject. "The sense that India and Britain are opposed nations...is played down, muffled, frittered away" (204), Said argues, and in its place are a set of philosophical questions that reinforce the racial topography of colonialism: the East as unknowable "Other" to Western rationalism. Thus for Said, Forster's Indian characters are less believable political agents than grounds for metaphysical speculation on the limits of the European mind: "Forster's India is so affectionately personal and so remorselessly metaphysical that his view of Indians as a nation contending for sovereignty with Britain is not politically very serious, or even respectful (204).

It's a fair assessment. Forster's India is steeped in Oriental mystery, a place where "nothing is identifiable" (91) and European rationalism comes face to face with "Ancient night" (80): "[men] desire that joy shall be graceful and sorrow august and infinity have a form, and India fails to accommodate them...at such moments the fate of the English seems to resemble that of their predecessors, who also entered the country with intent to refashion it, but were in the end worked into its pattern and covered with dust" (234). When Forster does turn to Indian politics, he portrays them as unproductive or trivial: "As long as someone abused the English, all went well, but nothing constructive had been achieved, and if the English were to leave India, the committee would vanish also. [Hamidullah] was glad that Aziz...took no interest in politics, which ruin the character and career" (114–15). When in the novel's opening chapter Aziz becomes bored by the conversation's turn toward "eternal politics" (10) and leaves to wander in the garden and contemplate poetry, this is for Forster a point in Aziz's favor.

But it would be a mistake to take the novel's disinterest in national politics as a disengagement from the notion of collective understanding and organization. Forster's attitude toward Indian political aspirations derives not from a suspicion of Indian nationalism alone but of nationalism as such. In his view, it is personal intimacy rather than national or cultural identity that should be the primary means of collective organization, a view that is not the avoidance of the political Said suggests. Rather, *A Passage to India* is part of Forster's sustained critique of collective identity in particular and categorical thinking in general. The question that precedes the novel's turn to "eternal politics," after all, is not whether an Indian nation is viable but whether an Englishman and an Indian can be friends. As Forster sees it, this is the question that most deserves our attention and the only legitimate ground from which collective understanding might be reached, and the ability to answer this question depends, in his view, upon the extent to which people can avoid thinking of themselves as Indian or English.

In and of itself, the claim that Forster values the personal over the political is not original. Forster is in fact explicit on this matter. His 1938 essay "What I Believe," for instance, places personal relationships as the foundation of his beliefs, even as it expresses his distaste for formulating a belief system at all: "I hate the idea of dying for a cause," he writes, "and if I had to choose between betraying my country and betraying my friend, I should hope I should have the guts to betray my country" (68). The novel articulates this same view on several occasions, usually through the character of Fielding, who is often considered Forster's mouthpiece in the novel: "I believe in teaching people to be individuals and to understand other individuals. It's the only thing I do believe in" (*Passage* 131).

While Forster clearly endorses such statements, one shouldn't take them too simply, any more than we should automatically identify Forster's beliefs with Fielding's. In both the novel and the essay, friendship and personal intimacy are not some easy antidote for political strife, nor is Forster suggesting that one could avoid categorical thinking and political and cultural identity altogether. However distasteful formulating a creed might be, "What I Believe" does take up the task; and neither Englishman nor Indian ever completely sheds their national or ethnic identities in *A*

Passage to India. But Forster also believes that human complexity usually eludes the ability of causes, beliefs, or collective identities to contain them. And Forster's depiction of India looks somewhat different in this light, for the indefinable turns out to be not just a quality of the East.

This last assertion is particularly true of "What I Believe," which, written in the 1930s under the shadow of totalitarianism, is neither apolitical nor concerned with the Orient. It does, however, insist upon the limits of beliefs and belief systems, and it is very strict on this matter. Even Forster's faith in personal relationships comes under the gun. "there lies at the back of every creed something terrible and hard for which the worshipper may one day be required to suffer, and there is even a terror and hardness in this creed of personal relationships, urbane and mild though it sounds" (69). The point isn't that one can avoid beliefs any more than one can avoid politics ("If a government cannot count upon the police and the army," he asks, "how can it hope to rule?" [70]) But for Forster there is always something potentially coercive in any creed, let alone any government, even one founded on the best principles. Hence his assertion that "two cheers [for democracy] is quite enough. There is no need to give three" (70). For Forster, plurality itself can become oppressive, the value that trumps all values.

In opposition to this generalizing tendency, Forster proposes something he calls "an aristocracy of the sensitive" (73), which at first glance seems an odd statement for an advocate of democracy, as he notes; but for Forster it is not wealth or power but creativity that characterizes this select group. In one sense, this is Forster championing his chosen vocation and the artistic cause more generally. But for Forster creativity implies more than just the making of art; it involves the ability to "make it new," to borrow Ezra Pound's phrase, which is another way of saying that the creative is what continually defies categorization. Indeed, resistance to categorization turns out to be the defining quality of this particular aristocracy:

> On they go—an invincible army, yet not a victorious one. The aristocrats, the elect, the chosen, the best people—all the words that describe them are false, and all attempts to organize them fail. Again and Again, authority, seeing their value, has tried to net them and to utilize them as the Egyptian Priesthood or the Christian Church or the Chinese Civil Services or the Group Movement, or some other worthy stunt. But they slip through the net and are gone; when the door is shut, they are no longer in the room. (74)

Invincible but not victorious: this is the crucial distinction for Forster. The oppositional nature of these individuals, their ability to elude all categorization, must remain intact. Which also means their particular vision can never triumph, for their special virtue is that they always remain outside any attempts to contain them.

Turning back to *A Passage to India,* I hope it's clear that while Forster may be absorbed in Orientalist thinking, his treatment of India in the novel is no mere Orientalism. Because in important respects Forster's India in which "nothing is indentifiable" is no different than his beloved aristocracy. "Nothing embraces the whole of India," as the novel claims (160); it always slips through the net and out the door. Thus Said's charge that the novel mythologizes India, or that it is "affectionately personal" and "remorselessly metaphysical," while true, is not quite the evasion Said claims. It is rather a different way of understanding collectivity, or, better to say, a different way of reaching it. Forster articulates this in the exchange between Fielding and Aziz after the latter shows Fielding a photograph of his wife, thus violating the restrictions of Purdah:

> "Really, I don't know why you pay me this great compliment, Aziz, but I do appreciate it."
>
> "Oh, it's nothing.... You would have seen her, so why should you not see the photograph?"
>
> "You would have allowed me to see her?"
>
> "Why not? I believe in the Purdah, but I should have told her you were my brother, and she would have seen you. Hamidullah saw her, and several others."
>
> "Did she think they were your brothers?"
>
> "Of course not, but the word exists and is convenient. All men are my brothers, and as soon as one behaves as such he may see my wife."
>
> "And when the whole world behaves as such, there will be no more purdah?"
>
> "It is because you can say and feel such a remark as that, that I show you the photograph." (125–26)

For Forster, one's success in overcoming such barriers depends in part on where you begin, which in his view should never be with the collective. To put it in the language of our conference, as he sees it starting from the premise of engaging worlds gets things the wrong way round. For in Forster's view, we need to resist categorizations, national, religious, racial, or otherwise, if we are to make any progress in finding our way to one another. This is not to say that he believes such a thing is easy or even possible, that we can conceive of ourselves without our collective self-understandings or avoid the realms of history and practical politics. Fielding, despite his desire, is to "slink through India unlabelled" (193), is more entrenched in his Englishness at the end of the novel than at the beginning, and his friendship with Aziz remains unrealized, perhaps unrealizable. But as Forster sees it, failure doesn't make the task any less imperative. "I think everyone fails," Mrs. Moore claims in trying to convince her son to treat individual Indians with kindness: "but there are so many kinds of failure" (53).

Works Cited

Forster, E. M. *A Passage to India*. San Diego: Harvest, 1984.
———. "What I Believe." *Two Cheers for Democracy*. San Diego: Harcourt Brace and Company, 1951.
Said, Edward. *Culture and Imperialism*. New York: Vintage Books, 1994.

Tapestry: Christian and Classical Mélange in C.S. Lewis's *Till We Have Faces* and *Perelandra*

Charles Fisher
Aims Community College

At first glance, Christian and Classical ideas are turbulent in conjunction, paradoxical in juxtaposition—as when fresh water meets salt. When successfully merged, an exquisite beauty attends, a particular pleasure in the reading. We need only look at how Renaissance artists, sculptors, and writers treated Christian themes in Classical forms to assure ourselves of this truth. In the English tradition, Clive Staples Lewis, one of the last Christian Humanists, saw the power of blending Classical and Christian archetypes in a way that dimmed neither but illuminated both, to the enrichment of Western culture.

At his death in 1963, Lewis, Oxford Professor of Medieval Literature and atheist-turned-Christian, left behind a rich legacy of literary scholarship as well as lesser-known works of adult fiction, such as the *Perelandra* trilogy and the mythical allegory *Till We Have Faces*. In these two works, Lewis, in his characteristic rich, robust, crystalline language, explores the junction of the Christian and Classical and invites readers to consider the cosmic conflict between good and evil, the pull between reason and doubt, and the internal, eternal longing of the soul for its solace.

Both works provide a stage for the cosmic war between Good and Evil through the interplay between Greek pantheism and Christian monotheism in fantastic settings. *Till We Have Faces* conjoins the Greek myth of Cupid and Psyche with the Judeo-Christian account of the Temptation and Fall. Its theme is the tempestuous relationship between the gods/God and humankind: the work reports the female narrator Orual's bitter complaint to capricious, silent, vindictive gods. Likewise, Lewis's "scientific" fiction trilogy plays out the Cosmic Conflict on Perelandra with Edenic parallels. Ocean-wreathed, Perelandra is "sinless" (226), refulgent, pure, active, fruitful, and innocent; from its trees depend low-hanging fruits and iridescent bulbs of fragrant water. Ransom, the human Christ-figure, struggles against Professor Weston, representing Empirical Man: "the idea that humanity, having now sufficiently corrupted the planet where it arose, must at all costs contrive to seed itself over a larger area" (226). Weston is the quintessential acolyte of spiritual Darwinism:

The majestic spectacle of this blind, inarticulate purposiveness thrusting its way upward and ever upward in an endless unity of differentiated achievements toward an ever-increasing complexity of organisation, towards spontaneity and spirituality, swept away all my old concepts of a duty to Man as such. Man in himself is nothing. The forward movement of Life—the growing spirituality—is everything. (234)

To Weston, evil and good are simply dipoles of a larger life essence. Quite Obi-Wan-like, he declares, "*Your* Devil and *your* God are both pictures of the same Force" (236). A megalomaniac, Weston claims for himself the scepter of the Force, without realizing he is simply, terribly, a tool of Satan in an Edenic *redux*. "I *am* the Universe," he proclaims. "I, Weston, am your God and your Devil. I call that Force into me completely" (238). Following this Faustian incantation, his physical features and voice metamorphose into a real, malevolent foe.

Ransom and Weston—the amoral, atheistic intellectual—battle for the soul and mind of the Green Woman, the Eve-figure in *Perelandra*. Ransom triumphs intellectually and physically, but during the prolonged grappling, Weston bites Ransom's heel, a wound that never heals, oozing blood for the rest of his life. The incident echoes God's Curse on the serpent/Satan: "[The man] will crush your head, and you will strike his heel" (Gen. 3.15).

In both novels we see additional parallels to the biblical account of the Fall in the strategies of seduction and persuasion. In the biblical narrative, Satan uses doubt and intellectual sophistry to entice humans to violate the one command they may *not* violate, on pain of eternal punishment. Likewise, in Lewis's novels, doubt-seeding and sophistry prevail as means of precipitating similar Falls. Psyche has been told by the Brute (Cupid) that the paradise she enjoys is conditioned on her never seeing his face. Orual, however, in her well-intended mission to rescue her half-sister, plants a seed of doubt in Psyche's mind as to the truth about Cupid. The god's dictum, Orual rationalizes, means that he must be terrifying and horrible to look upon. She convinces Psyche to shine a lamp on the god's face the next time Psyche shares Cupid's bed. The result is a thundering wrath worthy of an angry Greek god, and Psyche is cast from paradise. Orual's sense of loss and guilt is palpable and moving: "What came back and back to my mind was the thought of Psyche...somehow ruined, lost, robbed of all joy, a wailing, wandering shape, for whom I had wrecked everything" (169).

There is forbidden fruit in *Perelandra*'s paradise, too: Maleldil (God) commands the Green Woman, denizen of the ocean, never to tread upon dry land. Weston, like the serpent in Eden, reprises Satan's role by seeding doubt, engages in sophistic hairsplitting about this single proscription, and offers an alternate interpretation of the mind of Maleldil:

> "I have already said that we are forbidden to dwell on the Fixed Land. Why do you not either talk of something else or stop talking?"

> "Because this forbidding is such a strange one," said the Man's voice. . . . "He has not forbidden you from thinking about dwelling on the Fixed Land." (245)

Here, Weston plays the sophist and interpreter of what God *really meant*. Also, quite like the biblical depiction of Satan, "What the Un-man said was always very nearly true" (270).

In these two passages, parallels to the Garden of Eden are close. In both we see forbidden fruit: knowing good and evil in one case, seeing God face-to-face in the other. We see the same expulsion from two paradisiacal, eternal blisses. We see the same vehicle of sin—a Tempter who rationalizes disobedience and casts doubt about what the god (or God) really means by his injunction. One might say that Lewis invites us to consider how falsehood is often a bedfellow of truth.

Both novels explore perspectives of the sacred, the meaning of *holy*. For Orual in *Till We Have Faces*, holiness is a "holy fear"—pagan, noisome, dreadful, poisonous: "What frightened me was the holiness of the smell that hung about [the priest of Ungit]" (11). Holiness is "the smell of old age, and the smells of the oils and essences they put on those girls, and the Ungit smell" (43). The temple is a "room . . . full of spirits, and the horror of holiness" (54), "the reek of holiness" (62); it is "all holy, deadly—dark, detestable, maddening" (79). In holiness resides life and death: "The Divine Nature wounds and perhaps destroys us merely by being what it is" (284).

In *Perelandra*, Lewis's (as narrator and author) first experience with the chief *eldil* (angel) of Oyarsa (Mars) parallel's Orual's description of the holy, but it is a different sort of fear:

> My fear was now of another kind. I felt sure that the creature was what we call "good," but I wasn't sure whether I liked the "goodness" so much as I had supposed. This is a very terrible experience. As long as what you are afraid of is something evil, you may still hope that the good may come to your rescue. But suppose you struggle through to the good and find that it also is dreadful. (173)

Here Lewis articulates the strange dichotomy of human-god-myth archetypes, our sense of something or someone ineffably powerful, yet personal, in the cosmos. For the Christian, the paradox is expressed in James—"draw near to God, and he will draw near to you" (4.8)—but to approach God and not die, "for no man shall see Me, and live" (Exo. 33.20). The narrator's fear is not primal revulsion as it is for Orual, but the fear of Isaiah in the presence of God when he cries, "Woe is me, for I am undone!" (Isa. 6.5).

Soul-longing, a recurrent theme in Lewis's fiction and non-fiction, is present in both novels. Echoing Pascal's God-shaped "infinite abyss" (par. 4), this longing, according to Lewis, draws every human—knowingly or not—to God, a void only God can fill. It is a reaching out of both God to man and man to God. It is the deep need to return to the pure relationship between God and man destroyed when sin entered the world. In *Till We Have Faces*, this longing is poignantly reflected by Psyche:

It was when I was happiest that I longed most. . . . Because it was so beautiful, it set me longing, always longing. Somewhere else there must be more of it. . . . I felt like a bird in a cage when the other birds of its kind are flying home. . . . The sweetest thing in all my life has been the longing—to reach the Mountain, to find the place where all the beauty came from, my place, the place where I ought to have been born. Do you think it all meant nothing, all the longing? The longing for home? For indeed it now feels not like going, but like going back. All my life the God of the Mountain has been wooing me. (75–76)

Late in the book, in Lewis's masterful, eloquent prose, Queen Orual, successful but unfulfilled, reflects the longing and loneliness of a heart and life without God: "I did and I did and I did—what does it matter what I did . . . ? Sometimes I wondered who or what sends us this senseless repetition of days and nights and seasons and years; is it not like hearing a stupid boy whistle the same tune over and over, till you wonder how he can bear it himself?" (23).

So, too, longing appears in *Perelandra*. At one stage of Ransom and Weston's conflict, when the combatants withdraw to rest, we read of Ransom, "The chord of longing which drew him to the invisible isle seemed to him at that moment to have been fastened long, long before his coming to Perelandra, long before the earliest times that memory could recover in his childhood, before birth, before the birth of man himself, before the origins of time. It was sharp, sweet, wild, and holy, all in one" (244). One cannot read such passages in both works without contemplating the timelessness of humanity's great, teleological question of Purpose.

Arguably C. S. Lewis's fictional *opera magna, Till We Have Faces* and *Perelandra* ask readers to consider the duality of human existence and the common ground of Christian and Classical thought rather than succumb to the modern compulsion to separate the two. Lewis's striking definition of myth in *Perelandra* offers us a clue to his understanding of the counterplay in human affairs—and the reporting of human affairs in literature—giving readers intimations of the space between eternalities: "gleams of celestial strength and beauty falling on a jungle of filth and imbecility" (329).

Works Cited

Lewis, C. S. *Perelandra*. Quality Paperback Book Club. New York: Scribner, 1997.
———. *Till We Have Faces*. San Diego: Harvest/HBJ, 1980.
Pascal, Blaise. *Pensées* #425. Great Voyages: The History of Western Philosophy 1492–1776. http://oregonstate.edu/instruct/phl302/texts/pascal/pensees-/.

Part III. Modern, Postmodern, and Future Horizons

Butler among the Mechanists: Fiction and Nonfiction in the Evolution of Machines (*EREWHON* as a Core Text)

Dorion Sagan
Essayist and Science Writer

When J. Scott Lee kindly asked me to talk about what a liberal arts education meant to me and to briefly organize my comments around a potential core text to bring to your attention in this co-plenary talk, I was of course flattered. But I also had some trepidation. As it happened, I had been reading a book—a slow reader, I have still not finished—relevant to the matter at hand: Italo Calvino's *Why Read the Classics?* I have to admit that I was reading Calvino, whose vignettes span from the *Odyssey* to Ovid, from Stendahl to Twain, in part as a kind of advanced *CliffsNotes*, to find out what I was missing! To pick a core text worthy of being read above all others and by all is reminiscent of the madness of the lover, who is persuaded of the superiority of his mate—except for the promiscuous advocacy—let us call it nonpossessive love— with which he wishes us all to partake in the uniqueness of his special experience.

A member of the intellectually unfaithful, this was difficult for me. As a liberal arts student at the lowly University of Massachusetts, Amherst, I noticed a not-un-common phenomenon, one akin to reverse psychology: I found that I took special pleasure, not in the readings that were assigned, but in the books I did *not* have to read for class.

Reared by scientists, I became enamored of science's Blakean opposites, magic and philosophy. After college I plunged into deconstruction, triggered not because it was recommended but because a literary friend warned against the looming *madness*. This illustrates Edgar Allen Poe's idea of perversity and Henry Miller's advice, based no doubt on his experience with censorship, on getting someone to read a particular book: tell them *not* to, that they would not like it.

Indeed, I specifically did *not* major in English because of its core text canon, which I felt to be too restrictive. I gravitated instead toward Comparative Literature, which included courses such as Avant-Garde Film and Madness in Literature, where we read Euripedes's *The Bacchae.*

So, my expertise as a proposer of core text will come from a vantage point of irony if not game theory, that is from the vantage point of one who with the pseudo-elitism of state school snobbery rejects the popular and the canonical as an initial algorithm (needed for us slow readers). If, as Walter Benjamin argued, the work of art is threatened in the age of mechanical reproduction, I wanted the artistic, the rare, the unique. If others were not reading it, or barely knew what it was, and I did, I possessed something of value, something that was not reduced to the lowest common denominator of either the hoi polloi or the Ivy League with their canon. If everybody was thinking the same thing, no one was thinking; and if everybody started to switch to something else, it was time to switch again.

Of course, this crude algorithm sometimes tricked me into reading the classics. As a high school senior in Pasadena, California, I read *The Brothers Karamazov* with the advanced reading class—it would have been difficult by myself, and it was not a work high school readers were expected to read. When the class turned to Faulkner, I read a little and, offended by its seeming racism and difficulty, I begged off and, with the teacher's indulgence, instead compared Ken Kesey's *Merry Pranksters* and Charles Manson's *Family*, a good cult and a bad cult as I saw it, using Tom Wolfe's *The Electric Kool-Aid Acid Test* and lawyer Vincent Bugliosi's *Helter Skelter* as *my* core texts.

All this is a rather autobiographically obnoxious and long-winded way of re-marking the peculiar difficulty, the problematicity, of an intellectually excitable but alas slow-reading eclectic dilettante such as myself, with my peculiar tastes, to select a book of universal importance. How do we keep fresh and special a book that is supposed to be for everybody? One of the books I did read was Henry Miller's *The Books in My Life*, where he divides books into three categories: Books You Have Read, Books You Will Read, and Books You Will Never Read. Needless to say, the last category is the biggest. It is also growing the fastest.

As a writer aware of this problem, I consider myself a literary heterotroph. A *heterotroph* is a word from biology that means *feeding on others*, like carnivorous animals, near the top rather than the bottom of the food chain. It is for this reason, for example, that I like a philosopher like Jacques Derrida, who seems to have predigested so much of western philosophy in so many close and complex readings. But it is dangerous to be a literary heterotroph, as errors may become compounded and concentrated like toxins in predatory fish.

Deliberating over what to propose as a core text, I immediately had to reject favorites like Clarice Lispector, Charles Bukowski, and Derrida as too quirky, recent, or vulgar. You can see my problem: What I loved about reading was the spirit of rebellion, the intellectual thrills of voyaging into new territories. I had to choose a book for everybody that matched the advice of the wag who said: "A word of advice: don't give it."

And then it hit me: I would read *Erewhon*. Although Samuel Butler—who also wrote the classic post-Victorian novel, *The Way of All Flesh*—was canonical, I was excited, especially to read chapters 23–25, the text-within-a-text called "The Book of the Machines." Unlike many, I had read Butler's nonfiction, published at his own expense: *Evolution, Old and New*; *Unconscious Memory*; and *Luck or Cunning*, as well as a good portion of his copious *Note-Books*. Partly disciplined by my liberal arts education, I began reading Butler on my own from the complete Shrewsbury Edition, housed among the million plus works in the Smith College Library. I was turned on to Butler when I found that philosopher and cyberneticist, Gregory Bateson, Margaret Mead's ex-husband, had called him "Darwin's most able critic" (19).

Butler is for me a near-ideal case, a freethinker who was both critical and creative, a canonical writer who could write beautifully but also a gentle heretic who upset both the religious *and* the scientific authorities. Even editor Peter Mudford of the 1985 Penguin Classic edition ends his introduction with a sentence that includes the words "the intense dislike that Butler may arouse often provides the best possible grounds for self-suspicion" (21).

This is my kind of core text.

As a sheep farmer in New Zealand, Butler was very excited when Darwin's book on *The Origin of Species* came overseas. Butler devoured it. It changed his life, making him far less religious and open to new spiritual possibilities. It also inspired him to think about the evolutionary status of machines. Born in Nottingham, England, Butler sailed to New Zealand in 1859.

Four years later, when he was twenty-seven, he began what he himself considered to be his first mature writing on the implications of evolution. The writings consisted of two newspaper articles; the first, written under the pseudonym *Cellarius* and entitled "Darwin among the Machines," was written in the Upper Rangitata district of what was then the Canterbury Province of New Zealand and appeared in Christchurch in *The Press* newspaper, on June 13, 1863. In the article Butler, or his *nom de plume*, declared that a new kingdom had appeared on the surface of the Earth that had supervened the animal kingdom, just as the animal kingdom had overcome the vegetable kingdom. Humorously, *Cellarius* traced then-modern machines such as the steam engine "to the earliest primordial types of mechanical life" (43), such as the wedge, the inclined plane, the screw, the pulley, and, ultimately, "to the lever itself" (43).

During this age when the telegraph represented the epitome of technology, Butler foresaw a time "when all men, in all places, without any loss of time, are cognisant through their senses, of all that they desire to be cognisant of in all other places, at a low rate of charge, so that the back country squatter may hear his wool sold in London and deal with the buyer himself, may sit in his own chair in a back country hut and hear the performance of Israel in Egypt at Exeter Hall, may taste an ice on the Rakaia [a New Zealand river], which he is paying for and receiving in the Italian opera house...This is the grand annihilation of time and place which we are all striving for, and which in one small part we have been permitted to see actually realised" ("From Our Mad Correspondent" 196–197). Butler, in other words, had prophesied the Internet–specifically eBay—and virtual reality.

But we cannot equate *Cellarius* with Butler's full insight into the evolution of machines. In an article anonymously submitted to the same *The Press* entitled "Lucubratio Ebria," Butler took issue with his literary other. He countered *Cellarius* with the following argument. The limbs of the lower animals are not, he wrote, modified by any act of deliberation on their part but "by forces which seem insensate to the pain which they inflict, but by whose inexorably beneficent cruelty the brave and strong keep coming to the fore, while the weak and bad drop behind and perish" (48). In other words, the Darwinian theory of evolution by natural selection explained our remote ancestors, but this changed when at last "human intelligence stole like a late spring upon the mimicry of our semi-simious ancestry, the creature learnt how he could, of his own forethought, add extracorporaneous limbs to the members of his body and become not only a vertebrate mammal, but a vertebrate machinate mammal into the bargain" (48–49).

Man, Butler's alter alter ego argued, during his "gorillahood" (49) had carried a stick for so long that he learned to walk upright with it, and later he used it both to beat his younger brothers and as a lever. Perceiving the "moral government" (49) of nature, man began to "symbolize it, and to this day our poets and prophets still strive to symbolize it more and more completely" (49). Taking sticks from trees, using the arboreal environment as a workshop from which we could add to our bodies ready-made limbs of many types, we were able to epitomize the slow, Darwinian evolution of simpler creatures, updating our body plan not by evolutionary trial and error but by whim. "Lucubratio Ebria" contrasts the "machinate" nature of man with other animals such as the opossum, elephant, and bee, who has "never fairly grasped the notion of tacking on other limbs to the limbs of her own body" (49). No race on Earth, the respondent points out, not even the "lowest Australian savage" (50) is without tools; indeed, without extracorporaneous limbs men would not even be men at all.

Such interesting and prescient perspectives on machines, presented as nonfiction in *The Press*, were incorporated into the fiction-within-a-fiction of *Erewhon's* "The Book of the Machines." What we see and what I think is so admirable about Butler is how his philosophical willingness to play, to engage the ludic, to be funny and serious at the same time, allows concepts to bounce off each other and the zeitgeist to work itself out through him, as he fearlessly explores and alters received wisdom.

Erewhon shows the power of fiction to philosophically explore in a way more nuanced than the essay, with its single point of view. The drama and the play, the novel and cinema can enact a story without obvious endorsement of opinion. They can portray and play multiple sides, which is what reality does in the natural creativeness of its competition. In a sense, this is what Butler's utopia does—it gives several sides berth to interact and, if possible, battle it out. This is philosophical fiction, availing itself of multiple perspectives to keep the question open, rather than rush to conclusion.

In fact, one might argue that Plato's dialogues are essentially proto-novels, older than what is sometimes considered the first modern novel, Cervantes's *Don Quixote.* Nietzsche tells us that Plato was planning to be a tragedian, before he met Socrates and burned all his plays.

It is Butler's combination of open-mindedness and play, creativity, and critical thinking that makes me want to wholeheartedly offer *Erewhon* for your consideration as a core text. And it is not only the evolution of machines, but also the mechanical nature of Darwin's description of evolution and the nature of scientists—who Butler warned are "the priests of the modern age, and must be watched very closely"—that Butler explores.

In *Erewhon* all machines—or the modern ones anyway—are destroyed 100s of years before the hero arrives. The imaginary English colony is a strange mélange of social mores and customs, habits and ethnicities. It has gone through a period when meat is illegal. The hero's own watch is confiscated in a strip search. He is taken deeper into the country blindfolded. There he falls in love with the daughter of a man who is punished for being sick—as is the custom in *Erewhon*, where those who commit crimes are pitied and sent to hospitals, whereas those who become sick are held to account and sent to prison. The hero's possession of a watch is considered an infraction as serious as contracting typhus fever, but he is treated leniently in part due to his good looks and healthy head of blond hair.

At first in New Zealand, Butler was very excited to receive *The Origin of Species*. But, as he read up on the subject, Butler decided that Darwin had "taken the life out of biology." He wondered what happened to the non-mechanical evolutionists of men such as Lamarck, Buffon, and Erasmus Darwin. For them, as Butler put it, life did not depend just "on the cards you were dealt, but also on how you played them."

Inside Butler is a fascinating nuanced critique of free will and determinism. It is as if, Butler is saying, Darwin cannot be right that evolution is such a mechanical operation—but, if he is right, then machines must also be part of evolution. Although arguably canonical, Butler's imaginary anthropology, *Erewhon*, and his nonfiction works remain steadfastly rebellious, retaining their power to intellectually provoke and inspire a century and a half after their production. I recommend them for your consideration.

Works Cited

Bateson, Gregory. *Mind and Nature: A Necessary Unity*. New York: Hampton, 2002.

Butler, Samuel. "Darwin among the Machines." Reprinted in *The Note-Books of Samuel Butler*. Ed. Henry F. Jones. New York: Dutton, 1917. 42–47.

———. *Erewhon*. Ed. and intro. Peter Mudford. New York: Penguin, 1985.

———. "From Our Mad Correspondent." *The Press*. September 15, 1863. Christchurch, New Zealand. Reprinted in *The Cradle of Erewhon: Samuel Butler in New Zealand*. Joseph Jones. Austin: U Texas P, 1959. Appendix C, 195–200.

———. "Lucubratio Ebria." Reprinted in *The Note-Books of Samuel Butler*. Ed. Henry F. Jones. New York: Dutton, 1917. 47–53.

Beauty's Contexts: *Symposium* Then and Now

Mark Walter
Aurora University

It is now time to talk about *Symposium*—particularly about the context it provides for an understanding of beauty that has become canonical in the West, particularly because the establishment of this context tells us something important about both our assumptions about what we call beauty and the significance of philosophical discourse. Yet *why* do our times call for thinking about that dialogue? Why now, rather than roughly two hundred sixty years ago when Alexander Baumgarten published his *Aesthetica*, opening up a realm of thinking about beauty that could lay claim to being philosophical? Or why not roughly sixty years ago, when Clement Greenberg was claiming Jackson Pollock's painting would set new standards for what is meant by beauty, thus establishing a new role for the critic in the formation of those very standards? The reason is found in a growing absence, in the elision of the concept of beauty from the discourses surrounding artistic production and reception in our time. One can find this reflected in the institutions that are built around the art industry: recently, we find an exhibition that examines the concept of beauty in art, as if that concept is not a given, an essential component of what makes art art. Yet of course, it is now *not* a given, as the very existence of such an examination demonstrates. We find the absence of beauty from artistic discourse reflected in the very reactions to this disappearance: recent works decrying the "postmodern" and its abuses of aesthetic discourse, up to and including new manifestos condemning the supposedly postmodern jettisoning of the concept of beauty. These are symptomatic of an unease, perhaps over the loss of something essential, perhaps over the very failure to complete mourning something that is dead. As recently as Pollock, beauty had not yet died; today, it is perhaps a question of what is meant by its ghost.

But why *Symposium*? Here we find what should be counted as the first "aesthetics," although, of course, the framework of sensibility and its reception that determines that way of talking about art and beauty is not yet operative in that text. Yet it sets the conditions for such a framing of thought: in its recourse to judgment according to an ideal, in its denigration of the physical and its valorization of the concept, and in its reference of beauty to the concepts of the true and the good, *Symposium* establishes the conditions under which thought about the phenomenon will labor. Then and now, *Symposium* limns the horizons of what we have come to call—or perhaps have ceased to call—the beautiful.

I would like to call attention to merely one aspect of this text; even in this limited examination, I do not hope to do much more than indicate something that gives us perhaps one or a few questions to consider. That aspect is the re-contextualization of *doxa* about beauty in *Symposium*. More precisely, I want to highlight not so much the process, but a few of the conditions of Plato's re-contextualization of the meaning of beauty in that dialogue, toward the end of asking what that tells us about the fate of the concept of beauty in artistic discourse today, as well about philosophy's possible relation to that discourse.

Symposium is a dialogue about *eros*: first and foremost, its focus is on erotic love and the desire that appertains to it. It is a pious focus: eros is here, apparently for the "first" time, treated as a proper object of an *encomion*, and its divinity seems to be taken very seriously. It is also very clearly a dialogue about the *civic* significance of eros. This emphasis is very well encompassed within the conception of a divine, as the speeches of Phaedrus and Pausanius clearly demonstrate.

Phaedrus' speech quickly establishes that the key to civil life is the god-given phenomenon of eros. This is not a Promethean vision: unlike the *techne* Prometheus grants to humans, without which they could not live with one another, this is not a Titanic, but an Olympian gift, and thus a more properly *ordered* legacy:

> For the guiding principle you should choose for all our days, if we are minded to live a comely life (*kalos biosesthai*), cannot be acquired either by kinship or office or wealth or anything so well as by Love. What shall I call this power? The shame (*aischrois*) that we feel for shameful things, and ambition (*philotimian*) for what is noble: without which it is impossible for city or person to perform any high and noble deeds. (100: 178c–d)

Here, eros is taken to form a divinely-sanctioned link between a lover and a beloved that seems to support civic virtue with a deeply internalized emotional motivation. This is presented as the ground of not so much a capable or stable city, but indeed of an exemplary one, a dominant, powerful, and noble *polis*. As Phaedrus famously enthuses, "a city or an army composed of lovers and their favorites," however small, might even be thought capable of being "victorious over all the world" (102; 179a).

Of course, in an age of waning hegemony of the *polis*, and the veritable eclipse of Athens as the dominant force in the Greek world, these are significantly wishful claims. But the manner in which the divine is drawn in to a discourse of about civic life speaks not so much to faint hopes of political resurrection, but rather recalls the putative cause of political degeneration in the loss of conventional, religiously-grounded civic virtue through the morally corrosive effects of New Learning. It is, in effect, a pre-philosophical, pre-sophistic, and eminently conservative viewpoint, one whose civic erotics are outmoded yet still bear some ideological currency. It is, therefore, *doxic* in an operative sense—which is to say *incompletely grounded*—and thus ripe for the rethinking of grounds that is the very project of philosophy, Platonic or otherwise.

Now, Phaedrus' speech is very short, and does not explicitly treat erotic desire itself, taking up the story, so to speak, *after* the presumed attraction the lover feels for the beloved has taken hold and the love-bond has been formed. It is an immediate relation of the *effects* of love on the *polis*. In that respect as well, it is incomplete; without a reading of the nature of the desire that links man to man in the *polis*, the foundation of this connection is left unarticulated and invisible. It is *muthos* and not yet *logos* in the philosophical sense.

Pausanius' speech, however, explicitly addresses itself to the question of desire, and in so doing introduces a division in eros between "Heavenly" (*Ouranian*) and "Popular" (*Pandemon*) types corresponding to the version of Aphrodite at their origin. In so doing, he establishes a hierarchy of desire itself. While the "Popular" type is directed toward "the body more than the soul" (*ton somaton mallon he ton psuchon*), and to the female as much as to the male, "Heavenly" eros inspires lovers toward males only, particularly because these are presumed to have a "larger share of mind" (108–110; 181b–c). In this way, Pausanias' speech articulates what Phaedrus left implicit.

The specifically somatic component of erotic desire in "Heavenly" love is certainly not absent here—Pausanius spends a good bit of time working over a fairly tendentious defense of the ambiguities in mores regarding sexual contact between men and boys—but the focal point of the entire argument is clearly not in the realm of the senses. It is, like that of Phaedrus' speech, tied to civic virtue: "This is the Love that belongs to the Heavenly Goddess, heavenly itself and precious to both public and private life: for this compels lovers and beloved alike to feel a zealous concern for their own virtue" (120–122; 185b–c). And like Phaedrus' speech, it too frames the proper object of desire not in terms of physical beauty, but rather conceives his attractiveness to be found in a "virtue" of both body and soul. In fact, the uncertainty of these dual virtues—particularly those of the soul—developing or even persisting in the object of desire is enough for Pausanias to recommend that "green thoughtlessness" in a potential beloved is reason enough to have him lawfully forbidden as a object of erotic fixation, so as to better avoid the "sad waste of attentions" such a love-affair would involve (110–11; 181d–e). "Mind" is more desirable than body.

Neither of these speeches deal very directly with the attractive power of beauty *per se*, either that of the physical or moral kinds, yet they nevertheless present a conception of beauty that is weighted toward the latter rather than the former. The word *kalos* is used in the context of a "comely life" in Phaedrus' speech, immediately afterward (as "good" kinship or conditions) in a list of things that are not sufficient to gain that kind of life if eros is lacking (*touto oute sungeneia hoia te empoien houo kalos oute timai oute ploutos*) (100–101; 178c), then immediately after that as a substantive (*tois kalois*) signifying "the good or the noble" toward which ambition should aim (100–103; 178d). Later, Phaedrus makes mention of "noble deeds" that win the gods' favor, using *kalos* in this significance as well (*kala ergasamenon*) (104–105; 179c). In his own speech, Pausanias uses *kalos* to signify "right," or "correct" ways of speaking (106–107; 180c), often as "noble" and "right" with reference to conduct (108–111; 181a-b), "seemly" with regard to the action of erotic gratification (112–113; 182b), and "honorable," (112–115; 182d, e), and "right" (120–121; 185b), again with regard to erotic capitulation. In no place do we find *kalos* used to describe the appearance, either physical or moral, of the love-object itself. Rather, *kalos*, as "noble," "correct," or "honorable" is used in the context of relations toward that object and in reference to the civic value of those relations.

Given the perspective that both speeches assume, this is not surprising; in speaking of civic matters, it appears to make perfect sense to utilize the term *kalos* in this way. Of course, in reference to this we can speak of the dual significance of *kalos* in ancient Greek, and while it may not be a case of opposition, as would be the case of the term *pharmakon*, for instance, it would nevertheless be a mistake to regard the concurrence of frameworks of judgment about moral qualities with frames of judgment about physical appearances as a linguistic reflection of a simple fact. This is not the case; the moral and the sensual must be taken as separate, and notwithstanding the mutual applicability of concepts of order and harmony in judgments about them, these realms are separated by nothing other than the phenomenal division between two manners of appearance. And if the Indo-European roots of *kalos* suggest that a more direct mode of appearance is indeed the ground of this term—whether it be related to the appearances of strength or power—the metaphorical application of this term to signify an *inner* configuration of a human being is just that, a *transport* or carrying-over from the sensually grasped to the intellectually apprehended, or, in other terms, from the kingdom of sense to the ordered state of logos, which Plato is now suggesting as the grounds of the state itself.

With the final speeches, those of Diotima and Alcibiades, Plato consolidates this very transfer. I hope to have indicated that this requires that he first establish its grounds in common opinion: that is why the speeches of Phaedrus and Pausanias are wholly *doxic*: they are reflections of a linguistic use tied not only to the concrete life of the Greek language, but also necessarily grounded in the conditions that shape its being. We know that these conditions, in the fourth century BCE, could be said to coalesce around the crisis of the *polis*, precisely the issue of its justification, and more precisely, on the issue of consolidating and transmitting the values that would serve as its grounds. The *doxic* expression of eros in the service of the *polis* is, no doubt, part of an aristocratic ideology that would seek to "civilize" erotic attachments and which could be figured, given its androcentrism, to minimize any feminine "presence" in the realm of the state *per se*. Plato's presentation of this *doxa* appears to be designed to highlight those elements of it that can be best developed in his own re-conceptualization. The presentation of a *doxic* valorization of an ethical sense of *kalos*, a denigration of the feminine and the physical, and an emphasis on an initiatory conception of education all serve this end. And, of course, these all have an effect on the conception of beauty that emerges from this constellation.

In Diotima's speech, the penultimate stage in the formation of this nexus, Plato assembles a somewhat varied context from the elements of this *doxa*. And we find that here too, a consolidation of the conception of beauty is effected within the boundaries of this new context. The first thing to note here is that eros is no longer considered a god, but rather as an intermediary between the divine and the human—a *daimon megas*—the characterization of which frames a conception of beauty as that toward which this entity strives. He is, as Diotima states, "set on beautiful things" (*esti de ton kalon hos su phes*) (182–185; 204d), toward which he continually strives. For the first time in the dialogue, *to kalon* is explicitly conceived as the object of desire, as an animating force that draws or impels, and not simply as a desired goal or aim.

And now, for the first time too, the conception of wisdom, rather than virtue pure and simple, is connected to this interpretation of *to kalon*. "For wisdom has to do with the fairest things (*ton kalliston*), and Love is a love directed to what is fair; so that Love must needs be a friend of wisdom, and, as such, must be between wise and ignorant" (182–183; 204b). In drawing a parallel between erotic desire as an approach to the beautiful and philosophy as an approach to wisdom, Plato places the *doxa* expressed in the speeches of Phaedrus and Pausanias in a new frame. Erotic desire for the beautiful other is now not simply a means to effectuate a noble and good *ethos* in both lover and beloved. Rather, it is itself a yearning for something that exceeds one's grasp, a desire that feeds on another desire, that for everlasting life. "From what has been admitted," Diotima says, "we needs must yearn for immortality no less than for good . . . and hence it necessarily follows that love is of immortality" (190–193; 206e). The parallel between erotic desire and philosophical practice makes it clear, then, that wisdom too is oriented toward deathlessness.

We know where this line of argument goes: Plato's Diotima, or the Socrates who ventriloquizes her, argues that erotic love, properly practiced, leads to wisdom itself, which is now conceived in terms of the possession of "true examples of virtue," which win one "the friendship of heaven"; furthermore, the person who accomplishes this is, "among all men . . . immortal" (206–209; 212a). These "true examples" are the eternal Ideas, and intercourse with these renders not only oneself immortal, but places the *polis* that such values serve on the side of eternity, if not exactly in it. *Republic* will have more to say on this head, but the implication is clear: a new *paideia* is being presented here (although that term may indeed be a misnomer)—the path to the transmission of values that will ensure the viability of the *polis* is marked by philosophical erotics.

Plato has thus masterfully addressed a social question the *doxa* of Phaedrus and Pausanias implied, but could not answer satisfactorily: what is the basis of the values of the *polis*, and how can they best be transmitted to those who will maintain its life? This is the context of the discussion. But in doing this, the given understanding of *to kalon* as the noble *and* the beautiful has also been re-contextualized in such a way to make the conceptually beautiful the archetype of all moral virtue and all physical comeliness. What had earlier been a contingency of language has now become a consanguinity grounded in a particular practice of *logos* for which Socrates, as the model philosopher, serves as the standard-bearer. Beauty is now "rationally" equated to the Good and the True. Or rather, "true" beauty is equated to the Good and the True; the division between appearance and truth, which is mapped on the distinction between the sensual and the conceptual has turned beauty inward on itself, involuted it as it were, to the point at which the outwardly ugly Socrates-Silenus can become the model of genuine beauty on account of the "perfectly fair and wondrous" (*pagkala kai thaumasta*) images he bears within him, images which we can only guess to be ideal elements of the *sophrosune* with which a love-struck Alcibiades credits him.

I believe that most of this story is fairly well-known. Or, in any case, the manner in which the context for the concept of beauty is formed—the political exigencies, technological conditions, psychological necessities, and everything else—is not invisible to our thinking today. Yet, to paraphrase Nietzsche—*two thousand years, and not one new beauty?* What has *resisted* thinking beauty otherwise—*not* more internally, *not* more metaphorically, *not* more Platonically? This is not the place to take up such a question. It is enough now to simply point out that the discourses surrounding art often recoil from the problems inherent in the Platonically contextualized concept of beauty and thus understandably tend to set it aside. This was prefigured in the metamorphosis of the significance of beauty between Schiller and Hegel, for example. Two lines of thinking could proceed from this recognition: the first would be to affirm that contemporary art and contemporary art discourse have justifiably abandoned the conception that art is "about" beauty; the second would be to say that the contexts of human life have changed enough that our conceptual grasp of what is going on in art—and what is going on in the phenomenon of beauty we still might meet there—requires new consideration that might take us beyond a Platonic paradigm. Of course, one may seek what we have been trying to find in beauty elsewhere and avoid the struggle of entering into such a thinking; let us hope that many of us would not so quickly collapse under the tyranny of the path of least resistance.

The contextualization of beauty in *Symposium* rather clearly shows us that the significance of certain concepts owes as much to the discourse of philosophy—whatever that has meant or will come to mean—as it owes to the linguistic conditions that determine the use of a word. That discourse has long ranged itself behind a certain conception of truth that undercuts phenomenality, affirms eternity at the expense of becoming, and—perhaps—more often than not enrolls itself in the service of domination. Yet, however violent, philosophical discourse is a bulwark against another, more silent violence that is all the more pernicious for operating in the guise of nature. Perhaps part of the reason for the eclipse of the concept of beauty in discourses about art is the long modern drift toward various relativisms that would obviate the perceived necessity of judgment about things like "beauty"; this is certainly linked to, if in not in part a product of, ideologies (sometimes operating under the guise of philosophies) promulgating new horizons of "individuality" and "choice" so as to better consolidate the power of the market over human life. Because of its inherently *negative* power, philosophy remains one of the few possible impediments to a colonization of consciousness that is now relegating the significance of art—one of the pre-eminent modes of self-reflective existence—to a consumer product like food, drugs, and pornography. The question of whether or not philosophy can come to a thinking about beauty that does justice to the *appearance* of art—and thus also wrest the thinking of phenomenal being away from its conception in terms of "raw material" or "resources"—remains to be asked. Art itself, no matter how "conceptual," cannot adequately frame this question, nor should it necessarily try. The future of "beauty" is yet to be thought.

Works Cited

Plato. *Symposium*. Trans. W.R.M. Lamb. Cambridge, MA: Loeb Classical Library, 1991.

Descartes's Doubt and the Beginning of the Modern World

Neil G. Robertson
University of King's College (Halifax)

Descartes's *Meditations* often functions as a pivotal work in Great Books and Western Civilization courses: defining the modern world and articulating for the first time modern self-consciousness. This is certainly the received view, but more recently, scholarship has come to strongly contest this claim. For many scholars, locating the beginning of the modern world in Descartes is to be mislocating it; that beginning is altogether earlier, for instance, in the late-medieval nominalism and voluntarism of William of Ockham or the turn to the univocity of being in Duns Scotus (Gilson 92–121; Ariew 55–7; Gillespie 19–43; Milbank 36–54). Others have pointed to the Renaissance—whether in the cosmology of Giordano Bruno or that of Galileo, or the political and moral thought of Machiavelli or in the skeptical turn to the self in Montaigne (Blumenberg 549–90; Strauss 40–55; Toulmin 5–44). What scholars point to is a certain break with or dissolution of the teleological world of the Middle Ages (as articulated in Aquinas or Dante) that they see taking place in the late-medieval or Renaissance periods—a dissolution that Descartes is apparently configured by and working within (see Gilson especially). The result is that Descartes's standpoint appears as perverse and built upon perversity—built on a fundamental negation of and abstraction from a prior order of being or beings. So whether one is a post-modernist or a pre-modernist, the impossibility and unsustainability of Descartes is preinscribed by his thought's belonging to this later medieval or Renaissance "refusal" of a reality that exceeds self-consciousness. So we speak of Descartes's work as a "disengagement" or "withdrawal" or "enframing" (Taylor 143–58; Milbank 36–54; Heidegger 3–35). These terms suggest themselves when Descartes's position is seen as belonging to a more fundamental late-medieval or Renaissance stance where such a distancing of the human from a pre-given teleological order is in fact operative (see Robertson). From this standpoint, Descartes's doubt at the beginning of the *Meditations*, which leads us to give up all forms of knowing until we come to the *cogito* itself, can be read as just such a process of disengagement or withdrawal.

Now, in a certain sense I don't want to entirely contest this account, but I do wish to re-read it. To do this we must challenge the claim that the modern precedes Descartes. I think if we see modernity as beginning in Scotus or Ockham or Machiavelli we are not going to get the modern right—in particular, we are going to miss what modern subjectivity is. It seems to me to be right to say that in the late Middle Ages and the Renaissance there is a certain withdrawal or stepping back of the human self from a teleological hierarchy, largely Neoplatonic, that characterized the ancient and medieval worlds. In late-medieval nominalism, this human withdrawal from hierarchy is really a co-relative to a divine withdrawal. Then at the beginnings of the Renaissance, in a figure like Pico della Mirandolla, the human is found to have no place in the world, to be indeterminate and yet to contain the seeds of all beings. Here we can see a perfectly clear articulation of the stance of the late-medieval or Renaissance self. We can find such indeterminacy developing throughout the Renaissance, for instance in Machiavelli's *Prince* and of course in a series of characters in Shakespeare. The problem is that, as Pico brings out, but as is also generally experienced as the Renaissance proceeds, the indeterminate freedom of the human needs to return to the world to be given content—to become an angel or a beast. But what the Renaissance comes to see is not so much the beauty of holy ambition or the bestiality of worldly desire—but more radically, a total instability of all content in relation to this indeterminate freedom. It was above all the sixteenth century that experienced a deepening sense of skepticism and cynicism as it became more and more conscious of the instability of Renaissance freedom and humanism (Popkin 17–143; Tuck 31–65). So one is left with Montaigne's "Que sais-je?" or Francisco Sanchez's "Quod nihil scitur."

Those who elide modernity with late-medieval/Renaissance secular culture fail to truly underline this nihilistic result of the Renaissance. Certainly modernity, and above all the modernity of Descartes, is unthinkable apart from the failed secularity of the late-medieval and Renaissance period. But, what I want to emphasize is that Descartes (and Hobbes in his own way) builds on the *failure* produced by this withdrawal from the pre-modern hierarchical order. The new standpoint of these seventeenth-century thinkers is not properly a disengagement, withdrawal or refusal of a hierarchical order that is somehow still there—as it is for the Renaissance—but rather the annihilation of that or any other pre-given order. The truth of that order is known to be without foundation.

This is why I want to emphasize Descartes's doubt. The first thing to say about Meditation I is that it is taking up the nihilistic result of late-medieval/Renaissance secularity—that produces only skepticism—and it radicalizes that result, makes it total and comprehensive. The modern is founded on the despair in any natural beginning. So in the three stages of Descartes's deepening doubt we move (1) from sensation to common sense (the unity of an experienced world) (2) to the supposedly eternal truths of geometry and arithmetic and then (3) through an hyperbolic doubt (produced as many have pointed out by Ockham's God) to the dissolution of every given presuppositions, every given content. So the self cannot be spoken of as having withdrawn itself from some prior realm of beings; rather it has shown that there is no prior realm of beings—at least for the thinking self. Descartes's doubt is not continuing late medieval/Renaissance secularity; rather it is a profound critique of it and an acceptance of its impossibility. What Descartes points to is not that this failure should lead us to retract the development of the self that was initiated in the late-medieval/Renaissance secularity, but rather to complete it and in doing so, overcome it.

In Meditation III, Descartes uses the expression "taught by nature" to capture the way in which we can passively accept the world as it is given to us in experience (Descartes, 26). Descartes's doubt is the demand that we no longer accept being taught by nature—but what this means is not that we are withdrawing or disengaging as we come to no longer accept the tutelage of "nature," but rather that we are becoming active, becoming engaged for the first time.[1] The given-ness of nature that remains as a residual pagan element in late-medieval and Renaissance culture is here retracted. For Descartes, thought will proceed only on a self-certainty itself grounded on the perfection of God. From this inner self-relation, thought can enter into and come to know a nature that is present for thought. Here Descartes can know from within himself what is believed through medieval theology—that through an inner and complete relation to God, humanity can enter into and know nature without relapse into a loss of self or confusion of ends.[2] The inner self-consciousness that defines the specifically modern allows for a human knowing of all things within God, as Malebranche will later come to put it. There is not in this modern standpoint the opposition of late medieval/Renaissance culture, of a vanishing human knowing or freedom to an equally unstable and uncertain world, whose result is skepticism, violence, and nihilism. Rather, Descartes is assured through his purely inward relation to God that what he knows certainly is also true. From this point of view, nature is a totality of causes that are open to human knowing—and thus the realm of fate and *fortuna* is altogether banished.[3] Put to one side as inadequate is a Neoplatonic ascent of knowing to a unified standpoint beyond the division of knower and known. For Descartes, rather, the demand of certainty is to start straightway with a self-complete standpoint which then enters into the relation of knower to known, subject to object. The distinction of the natural and the supernatural, nature and grace, is overcome, at least relative to the objects proper to enlightened human subjectivity.

In Descartes's doubt, we have then not an example of late Renaissance skepticism, but its radicalization to the point that the very structure of skepticism—the withdrawal of the self from the world—is overcome. The only possible world will now be one in and for this self. Certainly there are deep and profound problems connected to this new modernity, but the crucial point I want to underline is that these problems are not to be equated with those that arose from the structure of late-medieval and Renaissance secularity. What I want to resist is the confusion—found even in those who are keen on modernity—involved in speaking of the modern as a stance, a project, a self-assertion. It suggests a basic instability, violence, and negativity at the heart of the modern: that modernity is being imposed upon an existing order. My argument has been that the modern is, in Descartes's doubt, built upon the despair of all such stances, projects, and assertions. As such, Descartes's modernity remains, even as it generates its own deep problems and contradictions, utterly unsurpassable.

Notes

1. The contrast active/passive is the crucially defining contrast of modern rationalism: see Spinoza and Leibniz on this distinction.

2. This is the result of the *Meditations*; see Descartes, 58–9.

3. This is the force of the argument of Meditations V and VI.

Works Cited

Ariew, Roger. *Descartes and the Late Scholastics.* Ithaca: Cornell UP, 1999.

Blumenberg, Hans. *The Legitimacy of the Modern Age.* Cambridge, MA: MIT Press, 1983.

Descartes, René. *Meditations on First Philosophy.* Trans. Donald A. Cress. Indianapolis: Hackett, 1993.

Gillespie, Michael. *The Theological Origins of Modernity.* Chicago: Chicago UP, 2008.

Gilson, Etienne. *The Unity of Philosophical Experience.* New York: Scribner, 1937.

Heidegger, Martin. *The Question Concerning Technology and Other Essays.* Trans. William Lovitt. New York: Harper, 1977.

Milbank, John. *The Word Made Strange.* Oxford: Blackwell, 1990.

Popkin, Richard. *The History of Scepticism.* Oxford: Oxford UP, 2003.

Robertson, Neil G. 2015. "The Originality of Pico's *Oration.*" In Richard Dagger, Christopher Metress, and J. Scott Lee (eds.), *Selected Proceedings of the 2009 Conference of the Association of Core Texts and Courses.* Lanham, MD: Rowman & Littlefield.

Strauss, Leo. *What Is Political Philosophy?* Chicago: Chicago UP, 1958.

Taylor, Charles. *Sources of the Self.* Cambridge: Harvard UP, 1989.

Toulmin, Stephen. *Cosmopolis.* Chicago: Chicago UP, 1992.

Tuck, Richard. *Philosophy and Government 1572–1651.* Cambridge: Cambridge UP, 1993.

Teaching Pascal in Modern and Postmodern Contexts

Christopher Anadale
Mount St. Mary's University

Pascal's *Pensées* should be included in modern philosophy classes, and in any class in which Descartes's works are taught. This conviction comes out of reflections on my five years' experience teaching modern philosophy to Catholic seminarians. The work we call *Pensées* is the published fragments of Pascal's notes toward an *Apology for the Christian Religion*, unfinished at his death. I advocate reading selections from the whole work, rather than the often anthologized and decontextualized Wager.

There are four main reasons Pascal's *Pensées* is worthy of study. First, Pascal has a unique concept of human nature. Second, and related, Pascal is acutely skeptical of the power of reason, especially in contrast to the power of imagination. Third, Pascal takes a specifically Christian approach to God, rejecting the abstract god of the philosophers. In all three of these ways, Pascal stands in marked contrast to Descartes. Finally, Pascal's work holds a special appeal for the postmodern classroom and the postmodern student.

Pascal describes man as a bizarre being unlike any other on earth, simultaneously wretched and great. "What sort of a freak then is man! How novel, how monstrous, how chaotic, how paradoxical, how prodigious! Judge of all things, feeble earthworm, repository of truth, sink of doubt and error, the glory and refuse of the universe! Who will unravel such a tangle? This is certainly beyond dogmatism and skepticism, beyond all human philosophy. Man transcends man" (34). The self-transcendence of man is connected with the role Pascal reserves for the human heart, a mode of thought which grasps first principles, which is moved to know God, and which has its own reasons that reason cannot know.

Pascal emphasizes the weakness of human reason relative to imagination. "I do not intend to list all the effects of imagination. Everyone knows that the sight of cats, or rats, or the crunching of a coal, etc., is enough to unhinge reason. . . . How absurd is reason, the sport of every wind!" (10). True self-knowledge, the perennial desideratum of the philosopher, requires that reason come to accept its own limits and recognize what is beyond it. "Reason's last step is the recognition that there are an infinite number of things which are beyond it. It is merely feeble if it does not go as far as to realize that. If natural things are beyond it, what are we to say about supernatural things?" (56). The contrast with Descartes's confidence in his own power of reasoning is very sharp.

Pascal often connects the monstrosity of man to the limitation of reason in his polemics against Cartesian and Jesuit influences in his own time. "Know then, proud man, what a paradox you are to yourself. Be humble, impotent reason! Be silent, feeble nature! Learn that man infinitely transcends man, hear from your master your true condition, which is unknown to you. Listen to God" (35). Philosophy leads us to God, but through the confession of reason's weakness, not through rational proofs, Cartesian or Scholastic.

Pascal's notion of God is thoroughly Christian, in contrast to the initially minimalist conception of God given in Descartes's most read works. The Cartesian "god of the philosophers" seems merely to fill a useful role in a metaphysical and epistemological system, and is a far cry from Christ the mediator and redeemer. Pascal notes the contrast between the God of robust Christian faith and the God who serves as guarantor of human knowledge of the physical world. "I cannot forgive Descartes: in his whole philosophy he would like to do without God; but he could not help allowing him a flick of the fingers to set the world in motion; after that he had no more use for God" (330). Descartes's reliance on proofs of God's existence in the *Meditations* also leaves his project vulnerable to collapse with the failure of those proofs.

In contrast, Pascal rejects proofs of God as too weak to assist either conversion or salvation, which both involve movements of the heart. "I shall not undertake here to prove by reasons from nature either the existence of God, or the Trinity or the immortality of the soul, or anything of that kind: not just because I should not feel competent to find in nature arguments which would convince hardened atheists, but also because such knowledge, without Christ, is useless and sterile" (141).

Pascal's Christian concept of God relates to the monstrousness of man, in that philosophers who approach God without the proper sense of their own nature inevitably form a distorted view of the divine. "Those who have known God without knowing their own wretchedness have not glorified him but themselves" (57). Students might consider whether Pascal, had he lived longer, would have regarded Spinoza's pantheism as an example of this error.

In the postmodern classroom, the *Pensées*, like Augustine's *Confessions*, may appeal to students experientially, as the sincere and intimate reflections of a seeker. Pascal neither creates nor adopts a system of philosophy, but struggles with the challenges and contradictions of the human condition as he lives it. In rejecting Cartesian innovation, Pascal does not return to medieval philosophy or theology. His thoughts suggest an alternative modern approach to philosophy, one left incomplete by his early death. Pascal speaks non-authoritatively but passionately, avoiding the hubris of modern rationalism and the dryness of modern philosophical religion. As one of "those who seek with groans" (119), he conveys a proto-existentialist sense of man as a homeless being, lost in the cosmos. "Man does not know the place he should occupy. He has obviously gone astray; he has fallen from his true place and cannot find it again. He searches everywhere, anxiously but in vain, in the midst of impenetrable darkness" (118).

Including Pascal as a companion to Descartes helps students to consider possible approaches to God, humans, and nature that are not realized in the main arc of modern thought. Though limited by its fragmentary expression in the *Pensées*, Pascal's rival vision helps students to engage critically with the Cartesian project, to identify and evaluate its starting point and assumptions. Considering Pascal's alternative, even to reject it, helps students to conceive of modernity as a narrative, and not the way things obviously and naturally are. Students could also profitably explore Pascal's influence on later thinkers such as David Hume and T.S. Eliot. Even students who do not share Pascal's faith may find in his work a modern philosophical Christianity worthy of respect. On the whole, any class that includes readings from Descartes would benefit from some treatment of Pascal.

Work Cited

Pascal, Blaise. *Pensées*. Trans. A.J. Krailsheimer. New York: Penguin, 1995.

Core Values and a Historicized Reading of Franklin's *Autobiography*

Vince J. Brewton
University of North Alabama

Ben Franklin's posthumous *Autobiography* is unique among his massive body of work in that he did not live to print, publish, and preside over its reception. Franklin referred to this never-finished work as "my Life." "Life writing" points readers to the eighteenth-century spike in printed "lives" just as the genre brings Franklin within the orbit of student curiosity, living as they do in an intensely self-regarding, micro-blogging age. I teach Franklin every year at a public university in a sweeping survey format with learning outcomes tied mostly to literary history and form. This constraint makes professionally challenging any attempt to frame the text historically *and* position it in a vital relationship with the, as yet, unwritten lives of student readers. The tension between the responsible study of history and the demand for existential relevance marks the subject of this paper.

The call for papers for the sixteenth annual Association of Core Texts and Courses Conference seemed to convey a gentle rebuke from the organizers: the core text movement requires a more rigorous grounding of texts in history, or what the organizers called "cultural context." To contextualize that mild reproach in terms of my subject, let me begin with a passage from the *Autobiography* that reads, "I have always maintained that it is necessary to prove that man is not even at present a vicious and detestable animal; and still more to prove that good management may greatly amend him" (139). Close readers of the *Autobiography* will have observed that this is not Benjamin Franklin but Benjamin Vaughan—from one of two intertexts Franklin requested the printer insert before Part II. Vaughan continues: "I am anxious to see the opinion established, that there are fair characters existing among the individuals

of the race; for the moment that all men, without exception, shall be conceived abandoned, good people will cease efforts deemed to be hopeless" (139).

Vaughan's concern prompts a crucial question for scholars involved with ACTC.
On what terms is it defensible to teach this or any text in order to model the "good"
for present and future generations, as Vaughan was suggesting to Franklin? On its
face, the advancement of knowledge, "science," and the reproduction of that new
knowledge in the classroom, are not coincidental with the transmission of "values" as we generally understand the term. Depending on institutional affiliation,
for some scholars there is no inherent conflict in this question: the transmission
of "values" is their professional obligation. But if liberal education is to be a global
practice manifested in institutions public and private, religious and secular, virtual
and brick and mortar, pursuing a comprehensive answer to the question is of para-
mount importance.

I want to examine the conflict between the professional generation of knowledge
and the missionary spread of virtue by reflecting on the premises that underlie the
practice of teaching core texts. The birth of ACTC in 1994 at the height of the culture
wars and the many intellectual and cultural narratives spinning out of that origin
cannot be assessed in this brief essay. Core texts, however, seem to acquire the label
"core texts" for at least three reasons worth thinking about: they are or seem to be
crucial to understanding a historical period or movement; they provide a venue for
examining issues and "great questions"; and/or they allow an intentional focus on
values and principles that institutions deem worthwhile. While the first approach is
fairly generic and "safe" from a professional standpoint, the latter two approaches
are founded on a belief that some texts more than others bear tidings of a shared human condition, and they are consistent with classicist Alvin Kernan's assertion that
the "power of great literature lies in its ability to portray feelingly and convincingly
critical human concerns in terms that do not scant its full human reality and its desperate importance to our lives" (104). This puts us squarely on "core text" territory,
but depending on the institution and a faculty member's career ambitions, a "great
question" or received value position may create conflicts with colleagues and current
disciplinary standards.

It is hardly news to relate that progressive-minded faculty who detect in the
slogan "Great Books" a cat's paw for unacknowledged cultural imperialism themselves conduct largely unacknowledged values instruction on predictable subjects,
including a transcendent politics of inclusivity, a transcendent ethics of environmental sustainability, and a transcendent intellectual standard of history, to name only a
few of the most conspicuous. That professional standards prove such a weak barrier
to values instruction in higher education should surprise no one. Nietzsche and other
philosophers of history have asserted convincingly that conscious encounters with
history always serve an agenda. Participants in the sixteenth ACTC conference are
invested publicly with values instruction too, though perhaps not limited to the above
list, with the importance of intellectual inquiry, of the freedom of conscience, and of
the dignity of every human being as indicative of these concerns. On the strength of
the admittedly slender arguments above, one might conclude that values education is
an irreducible feature of higher education at the present time.

Suppose, then, that values education is an unavoidable, even desirable, component of education. In the case of a reading of Franklin's *Autobiography* that goes beyond a "Great Questions" rubric and risks asserting that there is pressing human news in the text . . . well, what's the news? I would first spotlight two virtues—industry and frugality—discussed in the *Autobiography* and identified in the "The Way to Wealth" as central to success. I would add to these Franklin's wide tolerance and also endorse his intellectual cosmopolitanism: at home anywhere, interested everywhere. Last, I would commend the deep civic virtue evidenced by a retirement resume that included the establishment of a fire brigade, a public library, an academy that became the University of Pennsylvania, a hospital for the indigent, a city sanitation department, and providing almost single handedly for the defense of Philadelphia against the French in 1747. There's much more to like about the *Autobiography* (and Franklin), but these five elements are enough to consider when thinking through a values-oriented approach to the text.

The conference organizers at ACTC have rightly suggested that this reading would not be sufficient in itself and that the text should be placed in the relevant cultural context(s). But to supply even the thinnest historical outline to the *Autobiography* virtues risks introducing inconvenient facts and exposing ideological assumptions that "presentist" readings have obscured—in effect, undermining the rhetorical force of Franklin's "fair character." This is a risk that we have to run. Contextual frames are essential if we are to avoid hijacking the *Autobiography* (or any work) as simply a *pretext* for values transmission.

What *are* the appropriate critical frames, one might ask? To foreshadow my conclusion somewhat I will grant that a consensus may be impossible on this question, but with respect to the virtues listed above, one need not invoke Adorno's Dialectic of Enlightenment to grant that Franklin's industry and frugality were not idiosyncratic traits but coincident with the rise of modern industrial capitalism, a historical development from which the present age has inherited an ambiguous legacy of human exploitation and environmental degradation along with many undeniably positive benefits. In the *Autobiography*, Franklin candidly calls into question whether it is in fact hard work or just the appearance of industriousness that is crucial to success. Wilson J. Moses complicates Franklin's commitment to frugality as economic theory by juxtaposing it with Franklin's view that consumer spending—sound familiar?—was key to the nation's economic health (135–36). On the subject of tolerance, Franklin's attitudes typify Enlightenment revulsion toward the seventeenth century's religious and political conflicts, true, but contemporary readers may concur with Nancy Glazener's view that immanent in eighteenth century tolerance is its failure as a comprehensive ethos (205)—a failure spectacularly brought home by historical events since 2001. Further, Glazener characterizes Franklin's cosmopolitanism as exemplary of what she calls "interest thinking," which is to say the ability to recast forms of "belief and belonging" as "interests" separate from self-understanding (204), which is to say again, not specifically private virtue but a habit of thought inextricable from a particular historical moment. Last, the civic virtue for which Franklin is justly admired is inescapably linked to his social climbing, his civic contributions trappings of the "gentleman" he longed to be in the minds of his contemporaries.

These spot interventions with Franklinian values are hardly meant to "debunk" a life and work so magnificent; on the contrary, this particular exercise in cultural context is meant to invigorate the dialogue between careful history and useful virtue. In the remainder of this essay I want to situate briefly eight issues from the text in cultural context to determine which *Autobiography*, or one might say "whose," is at stake in a "Great Books" discussion that intends to retrieve specific values from Franklin's age for present use.

To begin, one can do no better than connect the dedicatory epistle Franklin placed at the beginning of Part 1 of the *Autobiography*, a moving letter to his son William, to the permanent estrangement of father and son over Revolutionary politics. Understanding something of this unhappy relationship would encourage examination of the various strands—personal, principle, political—that tethered Franklin to the Revolution. Unhappily too, Franklin owned slaves and profited from the slave trade: this uncomfortable fact needs to be located within a framework for understanding how the fine gradations of servitude structured social life in the eighteenth century. Franklin and a group of his fellow artisans met regularly to present and discuss papers—the famous "Junto"—a casual association that resembles mid-term study sessions (with which students are familiar) far *less* than it does working class reading groups (with which students are decidedly not familiar). Clarifying this affinity can begin a conversation on how Franklin's monolithic association with other classically educated Founders conceals the class origins that colored his entire life despite fame and worldly advancement.

Gordon Wood's recent biography makes the case that Franklin's failure to save an imperial relation between colonies and Crown shaped the message of Part 1 of the *Autobiography*. In Wood's reading, Franklin's reliance on "friends," favors, and royal prerogatives having been ultimately to no avail, he responds in print with a narrative that stresses "self-making" (138–39), as if to say to his son, do not depend on connections and patronage as I have done. While this frustrated Franklin is not the persona Americans typically take away from the *Autobiography*, perhaps the Franklin readers sometimes find cold and too calculating would be humanized by revising his heroic myth. Moreover, "self-making" can be key to unlocking Franklin's lifelong use of pseudonyms and disguises that taken together convey a different Franklin altogether—shifty, sly, given to false identities—than the confidence-inspiring Franklin appropriated by American financial discourse. Like Franklin's identity itself, the *Autobiography* is a variable, patchwork text, consisting of a letter to posterity, a converted book project on virtue, a summary of his civic contributions, and an unfinished chronicle of colonial history. The pace of classroom instruction can flatten these differences with the effect of presenting a misleadingly coherent text and a single, unitary Franklin. Attention to the text's motley-ness can help reconstruct a Franklin that is inconsistent, mutable, and prolific in self-invention—in short, a more human and plausible Franklin than is sometimes derived from the *Autobiography*.

In his coinage of the term "parallax zones," Paul Giles reminds us that cultural context does not require geographical proximity for effect and that context can and frequently does have global dimensions. The heuristic of parallax zones places Franklin within the worldwide context of British colonialism—not simply as a colonial subject. a "subaltern" in the lexicon of post-colonial theory, which is startling enough—but more accurately as an imperial administrator. which as one of two deputy postmasters of North America he most certainly was (23).

Along these same disciplinary lines. Wai Chee Dimock's notion of "deep time" offers a historically sensitive model for connecting cultural context across historical periods (757–61). "Deep time" enables a reversal of the usual projection of a retroactive American identity onto Franklin and instead inscribes Franklin's text into the present, which it already informs on many levels. one of which is science. The span of Franklin's life. as Joyce Chaplin observes, parallels the emergence of experimental science out of natural philosophy (63). Reflecting on the roots of contemporary science reminds us that Enlightenment culture—in the form of instrumental reason—forms an important historical depth of the present. Franklin's interest in advancing scientific knowledge was always practical. "What signifies Philosophy," he once asked, "that does not apply to some use?" (9: 251). Whether this is evidence of a unified sensibility of knowledge or not. it is a starting point for discussions on science and ethical responsibility that have never been more timely.

Like it or not. no account of Franklin's life can pass without considering it in relation to recent theory on the formation of the self in language. For most of his adult life Franklin occupied a uniquely totalizing relationship to the network of roles constitutive of print culture—public author and actual author. printer. editor. publisher. embedded narrator. embedded reader. and actual reader, to name just a few. By incorporating into his identity so many of the sites in the print network, Franklin makes visible a print cultural transformation that bolsters postmodern theory's counterintuitive assertion that language is a precondition of the self rather than a medium for the expression of a preexistent subjectivity without history. For all Franklin's vigorous extroversion (tiring just to read). his self-actualization was accomplished through an embodiment in print: he conceived his life as a book. figured mistakes as "errata," and fully exemplified modern subjectivity's complex relation to the technology of print.

While these various threads of text and context cannot be pulled together in so brief a space. they do bear witness to the fact that to historicize is to complicate interpretation by forcing the reader to negotiate meaning outside the sometimes-restrictive parameters of the book itself—and importantly on terms other than the reader's own. My somewhat eclectic attempt to historicize Franklin's "Life" has resulted perhaps only in the construction of an artifact of the present. Whose *Autobiography* will my students read? The text presented by the inevitably arbitrary frames I apply to it. Be that as it may. close study of significant books cannot dispense with the context of history. Michael Warner aptly observes of the competing print cultures in the early republic "every printed artifact came saturated with the distinctive qualities of communities" (17). Franklin's posthumously printed artifact is saturated with the distinctive qualities of the transatlantic print cultures that transformed the public sphere in the eighteenth century just as the rapid penetration of new media has transformed the nature of communication (instantaneous. continuous). reversed the logic of public and private (our thoughts are public via Twitter/Facebook. our physical selves are private). and reorganized understandings of community (everywhere and nowhere at once) in the twenty first century. Embedding significant books within historically appropriate but unfamiliar contexts makes the books themselves unfamiliar in productive ways, especially for our students and sometimes for their faculty as well, thus beginning the process by which cultural projection is replaced by the shock of learning.

Learning, however, is only the first step in education, and it must be pointed out that the phrase "student readers," with which I began, connoting tweedy seminar rooms and maple-lined campuses, can obscure a fact of desperate importance: our students are global citizens for whom the horizon of immediate contingency includes nuclear proliferation, potentially catastrophic climate change, violent religious extremism, rapidly disintegrating nation-states, and widespread economic instability. Each challenge to civilization in the present requires historical understanding that by itself may provide no answers. The risks of a "Great Books" approach are well known—ahistorical readings brought into too easy relation with the present and specific cultural norms masquerading as universals—yet if we fail to summon history to the aid of the present, the risks are without question far greater.

Works Cited

Chaplin, Joyce. "Benjamin Franklin's Natural Philosophy." *The Cambridge Companion to Benjamin Franklin*. Ed. Carla Mulford. Cambridge, UK: Cambridge UP, 2008. 63–76.

Dimock, Wai Chee. "Deep Time: American Literature and World History." *American Literary History* 13.4 (2001): 755–75.

Franklin, Benjamin. *The Autobiography of Benjamin Franklin*. 2nd Edition. Ed. Leonard W. Labaree et al. New Haven and London: Yale UP, 2003.

———. *The Papers of Benjamin Franklin*. 38 vols. Eds. Leonard W. Labaree, et al. New Haven: Yale UP, 1959.

Giles, Paul. "Antipodean American Literature: Franklin, Twain, and the Sphere of Subalternity." *American Literary History* 20.1–2 (2008): 22–50.

Glazener, Nancy. "Franklin and the Limits of Secular Civil Society." *American Literature* 80.2 (2008): 203–231.

Kernan, Alvin. *In Plato's Cave*. New Haven: Yale UP, 1999.

Morgan, Edmund S. *Benjamin Franklin*. New Haven: Yale UP, 2002.

Moses, Wilson J. "Protestant Ethic or Conspicuous Consumption? Benjamin Franklin and the Gilded Age." *The Cambridge Companion to Benjamin Franklin*. Ed. Carla Mulford. Cambridge, UK: Cambridge UP, 2008. 132–44.

Warner, Michael. *The Letters of the Republic: Publication and the Public Sphere in Eighteenth-Century America*. Cambridge, MA: Harvard UP, 1990.

Wood, Gordon. *The Americanization of Benjamin Franklin*. New York: Penguin, 2004.

Part IV. Challenges from Core Texts

Wordsworth's Preface to *Lyrical Ballads* and the Principle of Pleasure

Spencer Hall
Rhode Island College

In the summer of 1963, Lionel Trilling announced the death of pleasure. Well, maybe not quite that. He did, however, proclaim the "devaluation of the principle of pleasure" (79) as an object of desire in modern literary, aesthetic, and cultural life. Central to Trilling's argument was his view of William Wordsworth and, by extension, of nineteenth-century Romanticism as continuing the philosophical commitment to material pleasure that was an essential principle of Enlightenment humanism. Trilling was particularly taken by Wordsworth's "bold to the point of being shocking" assertion in the 1802 Preface to *Lyrical Ballads* of "the grand elementary principle of pleasure, by which [man] knows, and feels, and lives, and moves" (56). Bold and shocking, of course, because Wordsworth deliberately echoes the words of St. Paul in Acts 17:28, thus substituting for the omnipresent divinity of Pauline Christianity an inherent and naturalistic economy of pleasure as the ontological and moral ground of human life.

Wordsworth's rewriting of Paul appears in the eight crucial paragraphs added to the 1800 Preface for the third edition of *Lyrical Ballads* in 1802. Although the Preface, like the collection itself, may have lost a bit of the "canonical superstardom" (Gamer and Porter 34) it once enjoyed, it remains a vital core text, not only because it is the first and most influential theoretical manifesto of British Romanticism, but also, to quote the Norton Anthology, because it is "a central document in modern culture" (262). The appeal to pleasure that underlies the argument of the Preface—and of many of the poems in *Lyrical Ballads*—has not, I think, received sufficient critical or scholarly attention and provides an important perspective for students as they encounter this complex and seminal text.

The words "think," "thinking," and "thought" occur 73 times in the 1798 one-volume edition of *Lyrical Ballads* and 140 times in the 1800 two-volume edition, leading Michael Gamer and Dahlia Porter to suggest that the challenge to readers to "think" outside the box—outside of what Wordsworth called in the original Advertisement of 1798 "our own pre-established codes of decision" (47)—"can be said to embody one of [the collection's] central premises" (22). By my own cursory count, the noun "pleasure" and its verbal and adjectival variants are used some 37 times in the 1800 Preface and another 17 in the paragraphs added in 1802. Those numbers do not take into account synonyms such as "enjoyment," "gratification," and "delight." Clearly, Wordsworth had pleasure on his mind when composing and revising (in part from notes supplied by Coleridge) his famous Preface. In it, he challenges us to rethink our "pre-established codes" of pleasure, not just aesthetically, as readers of poetry, but ontologically and existentially, as "enjoying and suffering beings" (424). The revolutionary project in both the Preface and the poems involves an attempt to redefine (or reaffirm) not only the essential nature of poetry but also the very nature and meaning of human existence at a time of extreme cultural and historical crisis.

Students might begin their study of the Preface with these sentences from the Advertisement to the first edition of *Lyrical Ballads*, published anonymously in 1798, that were widely cited by contemporary reviewers: "The majority of the following poems are to be considered as experiments. They were written chiefly with a view to ascertain how far the language of conversation in the middle and lower classes of society is adapted to the purposes of poetic pleasure" (47). There is nothing especially new or revolutionary, of course, about the idea that poetry should provide pleasure. The emphasis, however, with which Wordsworth, now writing under his own name in the 1800 and 1802 Prefaces, insists on pleasure as *the* defining "purpose" or "necessity" or "restriction" (421, 422) of poetry is noteworthy. On one level, Wordsworth throws down a kind of "romantic" challenge to the classical Horatian model of "delight and instruct," a challenge in which feeling trumps the more traditional emphasis on moral instruction as the true purpose of serious verse. As with the Preface's famous definition of poetry as "spontaneous overflow," however, one must note the calculated qualifications that Wordsworth builds into his argument: "For all good poetry is the spontaneous overflow of powerful feelings; but though this be true, Poems to which any value can be attached, were never produced on any variety of subjects but by a man who being possessed of more than usual organic sensibility had also thought long and deeply" (175). Expressive overflow, he makes clear, must be controlled and restrained or, as he puts it in "Tintern Abbey," "chasten[ed] and subdue[d]" by profound reflection. The sublimely disturbing joy that the poet experiences in that poem is "the joy/Of elevated thoughts" (94–96).

Wordsworth is careful in the Preface to "chasten and subdue" his radical valorization of the pleasure principle by employing it in the service of a normative philosophical ideal of "Man" based on belief in an essential, enduring, and universal human nature. "The Poet," he says, "writes under one restriction only, namely, that of the necessity of giving immediate pleasure to a human Being possessed of that information which may be expected from him, not as a lawyer, a physician, a mariner, an astronomer or a natural philosopher, but as a Man" (422). Famously, the poet is described as a "man speaking to men," a man differentiated from his fellow beings largely by being even more "pleased with his own passions and volitions" than they and one "who rejoices more than other men in the spirit of life that is in him..." (420). Because the poet, in the act of composition, "will upon the whole be in a state of enjoyment... [he] ought especially to take care, that whatever passions he communicates to his Reader, those passions, if his Reader's mind be sound and vigorous, should always be accompanied with an overbalance of pleasure" (183). Man, as contemplated and represented by the representative human poet, is a being that experiences "sympathies which, from the necessities of his nature, are accompanied by an overbalance of enjoyment" (422). "Nor let this necessity of producing immediate pleasure," Wordsworth concludes, "be considered as a degradation of the Poet's art. It is far otherwise . . . it is a homage paid to the native and naked dignity of man, to the grand elementary principle of pleasure, by which he knows, and feels, and lives, and moves" (422).

Wordsworth's Preface helps to situate various student explorations. The theme of pleasure—and its relation to the idea of the human—could be traced, for example, throughout the long nineteenth century as it extends from the Enlightenment to the Romantics to Bentham and Mill and ultimately to Freud. The Preface is especially useful for comparing and contrasting first- and second-generation Romantic writers (not to mention for drawing distinctions between Wordsworth and Coleridge). There is much to be learned, for example, by reading Shelley's *Defence* and Keats's letters intertextually as responses to the Preface in general and to its constructions of poetic pleasure in particular. One might also ask students to view *Frankenstein* through the lens of the Preface. Wordsworth's striking juxtaposition of the poet and the scientist as representative nineteenth-century cultural figures on the basis of their respective responses to and productions of pleasure—and thus of their essential humanity and social usefulness—finds a searching response in Victor Frankenstein's manifest failures as a scientist, as a self-described "artist," and as a man.

Finally, students should study the Preface in relation to Wordsworth's own poetry. There are, of course, the hoary teaching points about language and subject matter that have been enshrined in generations of literary histories and anthology introductions. It is always interesting to ask students to do some formal analysis to determine to what extent and in what ways the poet's practice does or does not adhere to his own stated principles. Equally revealing is to contextualize the Preface in terms of Wordsworth's poetic development. One might, for example, link Wordsworth's consecration of pleasure as "our natural and unalienable inheritance" (423), which Trilling called "bold to the point of being shocking," to the poet's even more bold and shocking, even more radical affirmation of a conscious life in nature analogous to and continuous with human life, with pleasure as the elemental principle linking both:

The budding twigs spread out their fan,
To catch the breezy air,
And I must think, do all I can,
That there was pleasure there. ("Lines Written in Early Spring" 17–20)

Wordsworth's pantheism, if that is what we choose to call it, is grounded, I would suggest, in the perception of an inherent pleasure principle common to man and nature. As the poet says of the prophetic Pedlar in the unpublished poem later incorporated into "The Ruined Cottage," "for in all things / He saw one life, and felt that it was joy" ("The Pedlar," 217–18). I would suggest further that this early but most famous phase in Wordsworth's thought is predicated in part on the notion that pleasure can be self-regulating; that it can carry within itself the power to "chasten and subdue"; that it is, to quote from the 1805 *Prelude*, an "Emotion which best fore-sight need not fear, / Most worthy then of trust when most intense" (XIII 115–16). From the beginning, Wordsworth experienced a deeply felt need for emotional discipline and direction. The Preface, I think, reflects that blessed time, recalled in "Ode to Duty," "When love [was] an unerring light,/And joy its own security" (19–20). That time would not last.

Works Cited

Gamer, Michael, and Dahlia Porter, eds. *Lyrical Ballads 1798 and 1800*. Ontario: Broadview, 2008.

Norton Anthology of English Literature. "The Romantic Period." Eds. Jack Still-inger and Deidre Shauna Lynch. 8th ed. Vol. D. New York: Norton, 2006.

Trilling, Lionel. "The Fate of Pleasure." *Beyond Culture: Essays on Literature and Learning*. New York: Viking, 1965.

Wordsworth, William. "The Pedlar." *Romanticism: An Anthology*. Ed. Duncan Wu. 2nd ed. Oxford: Blackwell, 1998. 289–98.

Wordsworth, William, and Samuel Taylor Coleridge. *Lyrical Ballads 1798 and 1800*. Eds. Michael Gamer and Dahlia Porter. Ontario: Broadview, 2008. References to all editions of the Preface and to the Advertisement are to this volume.

Quantum Feline: The Prescience of Poe's Black Cat

J. Scott Miller
Brigham Young University

Within the framework of nineteenth-century world literature Edgar Allen Poe's short story "The Black Cat" stands out as one of the more influential, if gruesome, tales. It first appeared in the *Saturday Evening Post* in August of 1843, was praised by readers, and quickly translated (as well as parodied). Throughout the balance of the century, writers on both sides of the Atlantic found inspiration in Poe's story, some praising his dark exploration of the human psyche, others borrowing the unreliability of his rational-but-insane narrator. Baudelaire, a fellow poet, mystic, and addict, translated many of Poe's short stories into French and thereby helped bring Poe to the attention of a wider European audience. His contemporaries Mallarme, Valery and Rimbaud all found something about Poe to like and emulate, as did fellow writers throughout Europe (Vine 9–17, 165–175). Poe's influence extended well beyond the Western world, however. He was translated into Russian, found popular reception in India, and exercised a profound influence on Japanese and Chinese mystery writing from the 1880s through the late twentieth century (Vine 19–24, 135–162).[1]

I proceed on the assumption that "The Black Cat" is a core text, and do so both because of its powerful and long-lived influence as well as for its stature among genres that sometimes find less attention at ACTC meetings: the detective novel, the mystery, and the horror story. "The Black Cat" fits in here not because it involves the fantastic per se, but rather because those elements signal Poe's deep attention to philosophical matters. In fact, most studies of Poe focus on philosophical explorations, his influence on subsequent literary movements such as symbolism and surrealism, or questions of identity, man's place in the universe, and the power of evil.[2]

In this paper, however, I will examine the role of science, or perhaps proto-science, in Poe's story and suggest how prescient his mixture of reality and madness are in light of twentieth-century scientific developments. This being a relatively brief paper, I will end with more questions than I can begin to answer.

"The Black Cat" is a short story written in the first person. The narrator sits in prison, awaiting his impending execution for the murder of his wife. As he tells the story we readers are given a fairly straightforward narrative of events, punctuated from time to time with sighs of regret or short rages that reveal the narrator's unwinding mental state even as they build suspense. Originally a docile, newly married man of moderate means, he and his wife indulge their fondness for pets, including a black cat named Pluto. At first very affectionate towards the cat, the narrator succumbs to alcoholism and, in increasingly drunken rages, first maims, then hangs, the beast. Early in the morning after the hanging, he awakes to find his house in flames, and barely escapes with only his wife and a servant. All that remains of the house is a wall that contains the shadowy image and imprint of a cat hanging by its neck.

At first spooked by this phenomenon, he soon explains it away as the effect of heat and lime on ammonia given off by the burning body of the cat, likely thrown through the window by neighbors trying to alert the inhabitants to the fire. After a short while he is at a pub and discovers another similar black cat with a white spot on its chest that he brings home. Over time he develops strong antipathy for this cat (also blind in one eye) even as his wife's fondness for it grows. One day, going into the cellar with his wife, he is tripped up by the cat and tries to kill it with an axe. The wife intervenes, and in a rage he sinks the axe into her skull. He then schemes how to hide the body, and finally walls it up inside a false fireplace, covering the brickwork with a coat of plaster. He then turns to find the cat and dispatch it once and for all, but the elusive animal has vanished. Over the course of several days, investigators from the police search the house, and as they make their last survey he, in great confidence, taps at the very wall wherein the body lies. A high-pitched wail pierces the silence, and the men tear down the wall to find the cat, still alive, perched on the head of the corpse.

Subsequent literary scholarship has examined various aspects of this tale, predominant among them the way in which the cat serves as a symbol of the narrator's conscience, as well as studies that explore pithy dichotomies like man versus animal, male versus female, sanity versus insanity, and rationality versus instinct. Perhaps because the tale explores the extreme poles of human emotions and morality, it continues to enjoy popularity even today, despite it being clearly a product of a very specific time and place, and a particular (and somewhat peculiar) author. In other words, like other core texts, "The Black Cat" can sustain multiple readings across time and cultural space.

The tale contains assumptions and language that may seem quaint or obscure to us today.[3] However, it was equally obscure for many of those in other countries trying to translate the story in the mid-nineteenth century. I have examined in detail a Japanese translation done in 1887 and find several interesting accommodations or adaptations that suggest elements of the original that may require explanation to those who did not share Poe's cultural horizon. For example, the allusion built into the cat's name, Pluto, though obvious to American readers in Poe's day and even in our own, required of the Japanese translator, Aeba Kôson (1855–1922), an appended explanation within the Japanese text that Pluto was "an inauspicious name, Pluto being the god of the underworld in the religion of the Greek era" [猫の名をプル トウと呼びしが今ま思へばバ不祥の名でプルトウは希臘時代の宗教中にあ る地獄の神の名であったもの] (Aeba 130). In addition, Aeba also expanded on temperance overtones related to the evils of the narrator's drinking habit, down-played some of the Christian elements, such as notions of guilt and the idea of per-verseness, and expanded on a cultural analog: cat demons. Japanese folklore and theater contains the myth that if a cat licks a murder victim's blood it can transform into a vengeful cat demon. Thus readers of the Japanese translation would find even more resonance to the final scene of the story: the black cat, perched on the top of the victim's corpse, has obviously licked the wife's blood (or worse), been transformed into a demon, and avenged her murder by screaming.

So a late-nineteenth-century Japanese translation of "The Black Cat" shows that the tale sustains readings from many different angles. In fact, readers may bring to their reading assumptions or worldviews that actually enhance the original. I would now like to engage in another kind of reading of the tale that I believe can be equally fruitful, this from the perspective of twentieth-century physics.

Early in his career Poe penned a verse that he adjusted slightly over the years, a sonnet to science:

> SCIENCE! true daughter of Old Time thou art!
> Who alterest all things with thy peering eyes.
> Why preyest thou thus upon the poet's heart,
> Vulture, whose wings are dull realities?
> How should he love thee? Or how deem thee wise,
> Who wouldst not leave him in his wandering
> To seek for treasure in the jewelled skies,
> Albeit he soared with an undaunted wing?
> Hast thou not dragged Diana from her car?
> And driven the Hamadryad from the wood
> To seek a shelter in some happier star?
> Hast thou not torn the Naiad from her flood,
> The Elfin from the green grass, and from me
> The summer dream beneath the tamarind tree?

The sonnet is sympathetic to the poet who, under the rational pursuit of the "Vul-ture" science (whose wings are dull realities), is not left alone to "seek for treasure in the jewelled skies." In the final line Poe underscores the tension between rational science and emotional poetry when he bemoans the loss of his "summer dream be-neath the tamarind tree." This poem, composed at an early stage in his writing career, suggests that the interplay between science and art, the rational and the emotional, troubled Poe, and the fact that he called his final magnum opus *Eureka* (with its allu-sion to Archimedes) makes it clear that this tension haunted him throughout his life, and thus makes for a fit reading of "The Black Cat" as well.

The narrator betrays his trust in the omniscience of science early on in the story, hoping that his ideal reader will see "in the circumstances I detail with awe, nothing more than an ordinary succession of very natural causes and effects" (1). He thus reveals his own doubts about his mental state as well as his faith that objective readers will be able to explain away the supernatural elements of his troubling experience. In explaining the imprint of the dead cat after the fire, the narrator invokes science to calm his fears of supernatural vengeance, attributing the phenomenon to a chemical reaction. Here the narrator, echoing Poe's sonnet, uses the dull reality of science to neutralize the poetry (in this case, the emotion of terror). As the narrative continues to unfold and its creepiness increases, the coincidences begin to erode the narrator's underlying Enlightenment/Age of Reason assumption that everything can be explained rationally. He grows more and more uncertain. As his fear of the cat increases, he seeks to punish, then annihilate, the animal. I would like to suggest that Poe's narrator, in seeking to fix the cat's identity or destroy it, prefigures that same uncertainty underlying quantum mechanics, in a narrative manner of speaking.

Werner Heisenberg identified one of the mysteries of quantum mechanics as the impossibility of measuring an electron's position and momentum simultaneously. And in this story it seems that, as the narrator, using increasingly violent implements, approaches an understanding of *what*, metaphysically speaking, the cat actually is, he loses track of *where* the cat is. Thus, at the climax of the story, when the narrator ironically gets his first solid night of sleep after killing his wife, the missing cat is both alive and dead: alive, as we learn later, inside the wall, but dead as far as the narrator (and reader) is concerned. So Poe's black cat, at this moment in the tale, exists in a state not unlike a similar cat posited by Austrian physicist Erwin Schrödinger in his famous thought experiment in 1935. The cat inside Schrödinger's box, as you recall, is both alive and dead because, absent an observer, it exists in a state of indeterminacy, containing all the possibilities (alive and dead) but none determined until an observation takes place.

In Poe's story the observation happens when the narrator perversely raps against the wall; the cat screams, revealing its living state. The narrator, the police, and the reader all observe the collapse of the indeterminacy together. I see this as a kind of quantum narrative wherein the cat in the reader's mind is both alive and dead simultaneously until that narrative tension collapses in the gruesome resolution of the story. Poe's anticipation of the strange nature of quantum mechanics in the way he structures the narrative of "The Black Cat" suggests that one important feature of suspense genres is the giving and withholding of information, the indeterminate suspension of resolution. In other words, Poe's story reveals an early and powerful example of harnessing the quantum power of epistemological uncertainty, the stuff of all great mystery and detective fiction.

How does this work in the classroom? I am not sure, since I have yet to teach "The Black Cat" in this way. However, I do foresee that one might use this reading in several contexts: to explore suspense as a narrative technique, or to demonstrate aspects of reader response. The one I think would be most productive would be in teaching a cross-disciplinary course involving science and literature. As for the question of how such a reading might work within a core text course, I guess we will just have to wait and see, although the suspense is killing me!

Notes

1. See also Silver, Kawana.

2. See, for example, Bonaparte, Hoffman, Gargano, Halliburton, Reeder, Frushell, and Anderson.

3. Examples include variant spellings and his use of the term "Night-mare" to mean a spectral visitor.

Works Cited

Aeba, Kôson. "Seiyô kaidan kuro neko/Ruumorugu no hitogoroshi." *Meiji Hon'yaku Bungakushû*. Ed. Niwa Junichirô. Vol. 7. *Meiji Bungaku Zenshû*. Tokyo: Chikuma shobô, 1972. 130–40.

Anderson, Gayle Denington. "Marginalia." *Poe Studies* 10.2 (1977): 40–44.

Bonaparte, Marie. *The Life and Works of Edgar Allan Poe: A Psycho-Analytical Interpretation*. Trans. John Rudker. London: Imago, 1949.

Frushell, Richard C. "'An Incarnate Night-Mare': Moral Grotesquerie in 'The Black Cat.'" *Poe Studies* 5 (1972): 4344.

Gargano, James W. "'The Black Cat': Perverseness Reconsidered." *Texas Studies in Language and Literature* 2 (1960): 172–178.

Halliburton, David. *Edgar Allan Poe: A Phenomenological View*. Princeton: Princeton UP, 1973.

Heisenberg, Werner. "Über den anschaulichen Inhalt der quantentheoretischen Kinematik und Mechanik." *Zeitschrift für Physik* 43 (1927):172–198. [English translation: J. A. Wheeler and H. Zurek. *Quantum Theory and Measurement*. Princeton: Princeton UP, 1983. 62–84.]

Hoffman, Daniel. *Poe, Poe, Poe, Poe, Poe, Poe, Poe*. New York: Doubleday, 1972.

Kawana, Sari. *Murder Most Modern: Detective Fiction & Japanese Culture*. Minneapolis: U of Minnesota P, 2008.

Poe, Edgar Allan. "Sonnet—To Science." http://www.eapoe.org/works/poems/sciencej.htm. Accessed 12 January 2010.

———. "The Black Cat." http://www.eapoe.org/works/tales/blcata.htm. Accessed 12 January 2010.

Reeder, Roberta. "'The Black Cat' as a Study in Repression." *Poe Studies* 7 (1974): 20–21.

Schrödinger, Erwin. "Die gegenwartige Situation in der Quantenmechanik." *Naturwissenschaftern* 23 (1935): 807–812, 820–823, 844–849. [English translation: Trimmer, John D. "The Present Situation in Quantum Mechanics: A Translation of Schrödinger's 'Cat Paradox Paper.'" *Proceedings of the American Philosophical Society* 124(1980): 323–38.]

Silver, Mark. *Purloined Letters: Cultural Borrowing and Japanese Crime Literature, 1868–1937*. Honolulu: U of Hawai'i P, 2008.

Vine, Lois Davis, ed. *Poe Abroad: Influence, Reputation, Affinities*. Iowa City: U of Iowa P, 1999.

"… He winces not": *The Souls of Black Folk* as a Foundational Core Text

Page Laws
Norfolk State University

> I sit with Shakespeare and he winces not. Across the color line I move arm in arm with Balzac and Dumas, where smiling men and welcoming women glide in gilded halls. From out the caves of evening that swing between the strong-limbed earth and the tracery of the stars. I summon Aristotle and Aurelius and what soul I will, and they come all graciously with no scorn nor condescension. So, wed with Truth, I dwell above the Veil. Is this the life you grudge us, O knightly America? Is this the life you long to change into the dull red hideousness of Georgia? Are you so afraid lest peering from this high Pisgah, between Philistine and Amalekite, we sight the Promised Land?
>
> —W.E.B. Du Bois. *The Souls of Black Folk*

As Plato's *Republic* (especially the "Allegory of the Cave") takes pride of place in the general Western canon, W.E.B. Du Bois's 1903 classic *The Souls of Black Folk* is seminal for the African American one. Both works question the role of education in enlightening and shaping souls. Both see education as a steep and rugged path, suited only to those happy few with the brains to become the "Talented Tenth" or "Philosopher Kings." Numerous scholars, including Arnold Rampersad (Wolfenstein 155n13). Carrie Cowherd (Wolfenstein 155-n11) and Jonathan Flatley have pointed out Du Bois's Platonic and Hegelian leanings. In his book-length mediation on *Souls*. Eugene Wolfenstein points out that Du Bois read *The Republic* and

Phaedo early on: "It is difficult to resist the temptation of seeing Platonic leanings in his conceptions of culture, leadership, and spiritual life" (ix). Du Bois even shares some of Plato's blind spots on gender parity and class (cf. Walker 84). The main difference in *The Republic* and *Souls* for today's students is accessibility. The ancient Greek text (though nearly two and half millennia the elder of the two) is paradoxically easier for many students to read in a reasonable English translation than Dubois's 100-year-old American English prose. Students—even at a historically black university circa 2010—wince mightily at its allusiveness, and the demands it makes on their own limited background of reading.

My title refers to the very famous passage above in *The Souls of Black Folk* in which Du Bois walks arm-in-arm with some canonical Great Authors of World Literature (Core Texts on Parade) who are all welcoming and apparently 'color-blind.' It is a soaring, lyrical passage of great power and beauty, but it can also make a seasoned, careful reader wince at its countercurrents and discomfiting rhetoric. But before looking more closely at this passage—a microcosm of the larger work in which it is found—let us consider the importance of DuBois' *Souls of Black Folk in toto*. Why is it important enough to be considered "foundational"? What is it (generically speaking)?

Souls is, as Du Bois suggests in his introductory "Forethought," a compilation of eight previously published (today, we might say 'recycled') and four original essays plus one original short story ("Of the Coming of John") which is not particularly well distinguished as being fiction. (In the Forethought DuBois calls it a "tale twice told but seldom written," but he sometimes uses the term "tale" for sections of nonfiction prose, as well.) One can rightly get the impression of a greatest hits compilation whose narrative through-line is mostly accidental. But a through-line—however accidental its creation—there most certainly is. This "bellwether, . . . interventionist text" (Cruz) is unequaled in its impact on African American (and thereby American) letters: "All of African-American literature of a creative nature" comes from it, says Arnold Rampersad (qtd. in Gooding-Williams 205). Henry Louis Gates concurs: "No other text, save possibly the King James Bible, has had such a fundamental impact on the shaping of the African American literary tradition" (Gooding-Williams 205). It is difficult to over praise it; but, again, what exactly is it? Mary Martin quotes Shamoon Zamir who calls it a *Bildungsbiographie*: "a fusion of the history of individual consciousness with the collective consciousness of a race." Like other great literary works, *Souls* makes its critics articulate. Jon Cruz, who considers *Souls* the founding text of modern cultural studies, writes the following:

> [*Souls* is] an American classic heralded for its exquisite poetic and lyrical compression, its phenomenological punch, its critical interrogation of the darkest dimensions of American society, its skillful merger of social science and humanities, and its appeal to the highest virtues of rationalist faith.

Call it a "manifesto" (Gooding-Williams 204); call it a carefully conceived "parodic challenge" to the "slave narrative" (Rampersad qtd. in Martin 54). Call it a Wagnerian *Gesamtkunstwerk* (Wolfenstein 3); call it a work of "symbolic geography" (Robert Stepto after Wolfenstein 3).

Mary Martin has convincingly argued that *Souls* is an epic, that is, a "lengthy narrative dealing with grand and important events" in which a hero functions as a representative of his people and the "values of the community." She even finds a descent into the Underworld (the catabasis here being Dubois' trip to the Black Belt) and various catalogs of heroes (Martin 60). But here, instead of 'wily Odyssesus' fighting the Cyclops, we have the 'liberally educated Du Bois' himself fighting the short-sighted Mammonism of the New South.

While the passages on double consciousness and the problem of the color line are the most important for students to recognize, the passage on which we are focusing for this paper "I sit with Shakespeare and he winces not..." is perhaps the most germane to all that is said and done at ACTC. Throughout the first half of *Souls*—this passage comes at the end of Chapter VI, "Of the Training of Black Men"—Du Bois has taught us to value Culture—both 'high' (as in our passage) and what we might today call 'low' or 'popular' (though Du Bois would not use that word), both Black and White. Andrew Schreiber in his essay "The Folk, the School, and the Market-place: Locations of Culture in the *Souls of Black Folk*" says the problem Du Bois is fighting is that folk culture and high culture are "valued in contradictory ways" (251). Schreiber prefers the terms "vernacular" on the one hand and "lettered" or "learned culture" (255) on the other. The Sorrow Songs are the ultimate symbol of important vernacular culture. Schreiber believes Du Bois is calling for a marriage of these two, and indeed a related image of marriage is used in our passage. Du Bois wants us to eschew the third "sphere" of influence: market capitalism (which pays, I must point out, for the "gilding" in those "gilded halls" and all those great books in university libraries).

What's unsettling, at first, about the passage "I sit with Shakespeare" is that the "vernacular" seems to be here omitted—unless one makes the extra mental move to see Du Bois's black presence (moving arm in arm with the Great Ones) as Vernacular Culture's implicit representative. If one forgets to contextualize the passage in this way, there is a whiff of elitism about the intellectual soirée pictured.

Part of the problem is the rhetoric itself: "He winces not" first gives us the pain-ful image of the white Shakespeare wincing at his Black fan (He winces ...) and only then withdraws and negates the painful sight by adding "not." The negation, in such a case, is never, of course, complete; the figurative 'erasure' of the painful word "wince" (we generally "wince" in pain) is never complete. We are left in the unen-viable position of being grateful to the Great Authors for not doing what we fully expected them to do, i.e., "wince" at the Black face of Du Bois.

Jon Flatley points out that there are no Americans (except the Du Bois persona himself) in the little Pantheon of authors Du Bois gives here: Shakespeare is British; Balzac is a monarchist Frenchman; Dumas is another Frenchman of famously mixed race. To find his next authors, Du Bois moves southward to the Mediterranean and back in time to the classics. He summons Aristotle (a foreigner himself in Athens) and Aurelius. Plato, Aristotle's teacher, and Plato's teacher Socrates have also come joined the little crowd at the mention of the "caves" of evening (cf. the Allegory of the Cave). Note that now the Du Bois persona is taking the more active role of "sum-moning" the dead authors from their graves, much in the manner of Faust conjuring up his famous heroes and heroines (e.g., Helen of Troy). So the German Goethe, a well-known influencer of Du Bois, can be imagined joining the Pantheon. They all come "graciously with no scorn nor condescension." One is brought back to the rhetorical dilemma of "winces not." Why mention scorn and condescension, only to negate them? The answer is clearly that the Du Bois persona has come to *expect* ill treatment from virtually all, and is therefore gratefully surprised when it doesn't materialize. The source of this troubling racial insecurity is all too clear: it is "knightly America" with that phrase's clear reverberations of the Confederacy's Lost Cause and its surrounding feudal mythology. Elsewhere in *Souls*, DuBois has intimated that the Old South did have some touch of nobility, but only in comparison with the New South's Mammonistic greed and materialism.

Then Du Bois shifts imagistic gears, rather suddenly, away from the gilded hall and strolling smiling men and women (either the Great Male Authors' dates for the soirée or—I would prefer to think—Great Female Authors) to the mountainous landscape of the Hebrew Exodus. The analogy between the Africans enslaved in America and the Jews enslaved in Egypt is a familiar, time-honored one. Both peoples have had to suffer their wandering years, as Du Bois has suggested, waiting for the manna of Justice or entrance into the Promised Land of Equality. Du Bois's mention of the Philistines is not merely a geographical reference to the story of where Moses looked down into the Promised Land. It is Philistinism (in its figurative, modern sense of 'ignorant hostility to culture') that Du Bois fears in the coming New South.

Du Bois's turn to a series of three rhetorical questions at the end of this passage (also the coda for Chapter VI) reminds us of a continuing issue here and throughout the text. To whom are these questions addressed? To whom, exactly, is the Du Bois persona speaking? The most obvious answer is that he clearly addresses the recalcitrant, racist 'knightly Americans' who might deny the Talented Tenth their longed-for education, artificially keeping them 'hewers of wood and drawers of water' (Du Bois 136). The "dull red hideousness of Georgia" conjures up young men of potential brilliance scratching away at the red Georgia clay—sharecroppers for life, permanently chained to the wall of Plato's cave. Hideous indeed. But there are other targets for Du Bois's righteous indignation, including all the faint-of-heart readers, White and Black, unwilling to make with him the ascent to the mountaintop ("wed with Truth I dwell above the Veil").

Reading *The Souls of Black Folk* today demands precisely the education in classic core texts that DuBois is himself *performing* in his text and *demanding* for his Talented Tenth. The irony is that today such learning, though more widely available to more people, seems to attract so few with Du Bois's passion for learning. Perhaps seduced by golden apples, fewer students choose rigorous liberal arts curricula, even at the Black colleges Du Bois loved so dearly and so well. For those who can understand Du Bois's hard-won language of shared allusions to core texts and his mastery of Western as well as African American culture, we can repeat his warning to all those so dangerously distracted by materialism: "Fly, my maiden, fly, for yonder comes Hippomenes!"

Works Cited

Cruz, Jon. "The Souls of Black Folk and American Cultural Studies." *European Journal of Cultural Studies* 7 (2004): 135–142.

Du Bois, W.E.B. *The Souls of Black Folk.* New York: Signet Classic, 1982.

Flatley, Jonathan. *Affective Mapping: Melancholia and the Politics of Modernism.* Cambridge, MA: Harvard UP, 2008.

Gooding-Williams, Robert, and Dwight A McBride, ed. "100 Years of *The Souls of Black Folk: A Celebration of W. E. B. Du Bois.*" *Public Culture* (Spring 2005): 203–338.

Martin, Mary. "Du Bois's The Souls of Black Folk and the Epic Tradition." *CEA Magazine: A Journal of the College English Association,* Middle Atlantic Group 17: 53–63. http://go.galegroup.com/ps/1.do?&id=GALE%7CN2812267 328&v=2.1&u=viva nsi&it=r&p=MLA&sw=w/. Accessed March 27, 2010.

Schreiber, Andrew. "The Folk, the School, and the Marketplace: Locations of Culture in The Souls of Black Folk." *Post Bellum, Pre-Harlem: African American Literature and Culture 1877–1919.* Eds. Barbara McCaskill and Caroline Gebhard. New York: NYU P, 2006. 250–267.

Walker, Corey D.B. "Modernity in Black: Du Bois and the (Re) Construction of Black Identity in The Souls of Black Folk." *Philosophia Africana* 7.1 (2004).

Wolfenstein, Eugene Victor. *A Gift of the Spirit: Reading The Souls of Black Folk.* Ithaca: Cornell UP, 2007.

A Journey to Self: A Psychological Analysis of Fauset's *Plum Bun: A Novel Without a Moral*

Karen Y. Holmes
Norfolk State University

Plum Bun: A Novel Without a Moral immerses students in the richness and diversity of early twentieth-century American culture while opening their minds to the complexities of human thought and motivation through the perilous journey of a light-skinned African American woman who, bowed by the pressures of racism, forsakes her African American family and heritage to "pass for white." A superficial examination of this work suggests yet another trite retelling of the story of the "tragic mulatto." However, a deeper analysis of this work highlights the growth of the protagonist from a fragile psyche initially shaped by the moral and social mores of the day, to a maturing character with a renewed sense of self who comes to accept herself and her place in the larger society. Students may bristle at the seemingly outdated pastime of "passing" and question the relevance of this text to the field of psychology. But a thorough critique of this novel reveals a rich psychological tale that demonstrates the timeless relevance of Jessie Redmon Fauset's work. With this in mind, I briefly discuss three key areas of interest: (1) the relevance of *Plum Bum* as a core text for teaching psychological theory; (2) the incorporation of an African American core text into a capstone course; and (3) the relevance of core texts for students at Historically Black Colleges and Universities.

In *Plum Bun*, Fauset crafts a tale of contrasts: a story of expectations won and lost, of dreams fulfilled and dreams deferred, of opportunism and humanity. The novel's title alludes to this dichotomy and frames the five books ("Home," "Market," "Plum Bun," "Home Again," and "Market Is Done") that propel Angela's story.

To market, to market to buy a plum bum, home again, home again, market is done.

The symbolism of this verse is telling. The gaiety and lightheartedness of this nursery rhyme stands in stark contrast to the sedateness of an economic transaction (McDowell, xvi). This verse provides a foreshadowing of the tension that arises between Angela Murray's desire for respectability, security, and acceptance through complete assimilation into the dominant white society, and the pull of her African American heritage and love for her darker-skinned sister. Only when this internal struggle is resolved can Angela achieve psychological completeness.

The novel's subtitle, *a novel without a moral,* again represents a contradiction in terms. On the one hand, Fauset's composition evokes feelings of spiritual loss, of a moral center that has been decimated by unremitting racial abhorrence and rejection; a fractured sense of self, searching for wholeness; and as we will soon see, friendship, love, and Angela's very identity seemingly "for sale." On the other hand, the deftness of Fauset's writing makes it clear that Angela's journey is not a smooth one and that there are many life lessons to be learned. This contradiction plays out in the five books that follow and detail Angela's journey to a reexamination of self.

The first book, "Home," introduces readers to the Murray family—a middleclass, African American family in 1920s Philadelphia. The story is told from the vantage point of Angela Murray, a light-skinned African American adolescent discontented with her station in life; as she feels that if it were not for the racial policies of the day, she would be amongst the intellectual and artistic elite. Angela learns the harsh realities of the racial policies of the day through several instances in which success and acceptance, thought to be hers, were cruelly snatched away upon revelation of her true racial identity.

This book highlights Angela's psychic struggle with internal and external forces beyond her control. Various psychological theories are relevant here; however, the work of Karen Horney is particularly germane. Horney suggests that individuals seek security in three ways: we move towards people in an attempt to seek affection and acceptance from others; we move away from people by striving for independence, privacy and self-reliance; or we move against people by trying to gain control or power over others. Emotional stability requires a balance among the three styles. Angela, in her pursuit of security and acceptance from white society, abandons her Black self in favor of a white mask. Angela eagerly moves towards whiteness, and further away from the true self.

In the second book, "Market," Angela leaves Philadelphia following the untimely deaths of her parents and travels to New York City; in so doing, completely rejecting her African American heritage and fully embracing her white persona. She joins an artist circle and beings a relationship with Roger Fielding, a wealthy white and racist suitor whom she quickly desires as her husband. However, the relationship soon deteriorates, as it is based upon layer upon layer of deception. Angela's duplicity is imbedded within her denial of her true identity. A stark example of this is Angela's rejection of her darker-skinned sister, Virginia. When attempting to meet her at the train station, Angela spots Roger, who was arriving home from a business trip; fearing his reaction, Angela walks past Jinny, leaving her standing alone in the crowd.

Roger and Angela's deception continues throughout Book Three, "Plum Bun." The lovers continue to use one another for personal gain: Angela's search for financial security and social acceptance is outdone only by Roger's pursuit of uncommitted sex. Deborah McDowell proposes that Roger and Angela's relationship is little more than an economic exchange, two people going to market to "buy" two completely different commodities: Angela, power, influence, and security, achieved through marriage; Roger, power and control, achieved through sexual gratification (xix).

This book concludes with a cooling of the relationship. Angela quickly realizes that she will be unable to use her "feminine powers of persuasion" to seduce Roger into marriage and succumbs to his advances, in essence "giving away" what she so eagerly attempted to broker.

These two books highlight Angela's continued self-identification as a white woman and her rejection of her Black self. But she also describes the stark differences between males and females in relationship situations. Many psychological theories are relevant here; however, I will briefly discuss the cognitive development theory. According to this theory, social learning is a part of gender role development, and involves the processing of information about the world and creating internal cognitive rules for engaging in appropriate behaviors for males and females. On the basis of these rules, individuals form gender schemas of how they should act. This psychological process is evident in Angela and Roger's differing perceptions and expectations of appropriate behavior in an interpersonal relationship. Angela holds to the belief that as a proper lady she should not engage in indiscriminate sexual activity and that a man must "pay" for his desires through marriage. Roger maintains that as a man, it is his prerogative to "buy" the gratification that he desires, by offering gifts, trinkets, and money.

"Home Again," Book Four, details how the ending of her relationship with Roger fosters in Angela a more mature attitude concerning the relationships between men and women. However, Angela remains true to the notion that she needs the security and acceptance that can be achieved only through marriage to a White man. She turns to her old circle of friends…and to Anthony Cross, who unbeknownst to everyone is of mixed heritage. Believing love and marriage are finally hers, Angela reveals her true identify to Anthony only to be crushed once more when told of his pending engagement.

"Market Is Done," the fifth and final book, offers a clear sense of Angela's development. Angela once again comes face to face with bigotry, when Ms. Powell, a Black woman whom she admires, is denied an award because of her race. Once again, Angela must decide if she will deny her Blackness as she did with Jinny, or embrace her heritage. This time, Angela reveals her true identity and stands in support of Ms. Powell. Coming to terms with the deceptions that controlled her life and temporarily estranged her from her sister Jinny, Angela begins to embrace her Black identity and her independence. The novel concludes with the unexpected reunion of Angela and Anthony. Market is done.

These last two books clearly illustrate the psychological growth and development of Angela. A coherent and stable sense of self has developed, shaped through changing attitudes, experiences, and critical self-assessment.

The previous review highlights Plum Bun's relevance as a core text to teach psychological concepts. Let me now turn to a brief discussion of how this text can be incorporated into a capstone course. Initially, the course would be incorporated into an existing core course—the senior seminar. As originally constituted, this course is a one-semester, six hour per week course that requires students to review and integrate the knowledge and skills learned throughout their matriculation as psychology students. This course not only provides students with a unique learning experience, but also provides faculty with a means to determine whether or not the learning objectives that have been outlined by the department and the university have been met.

The goals of the proposed core-text capstone course are several: (1) to introduce students to the broad scope of the field of psychology; (2) to develop in students the critical intellectual skills—reading, writing, speaking, quantitative ability, and critical thinking that are essential for mastery of psychological concepts, and for continued learning outside of a university setting; and (3) to broaden students' perspectives regarding the larger society, with emphasis on understanding viewpoints that are at variance with one's own. Achieving these objectives will enable students to develop their own goals, values, and perspectives and facilitate their progression into reflective life-long learners.

These goals will be accomplished through a series of projects that will require students to demonstrate their understanding of the core text and their mastery of psychological concepts. Project One would assess students' knowledge of social psychological theory. This project will require students to read Kenneth and Mamie Clark's classic "Doll Studies" and examine the role classical conditioning of racial prejudice and stereotyping may have played in Angela's decision to reject her Blackness and pass for white. Students would be required to present their work in the form of a multimedia presentation.

A second project would examine students' understanding of theories of personality and development. Specifically, students would be required to compare and contrast the personality theories of Erikson and Marcia. Students would pay special attention to the similarities and differences in these theorists' conceptualizations of identity. They would then discuss the relevance of these theories to the self-development exhibited by Angela Murray.

A third project would require students to debate the pros and cons of Angela Murray's decision to pass for white. This debate will be embedded within relevant psychological theory.

The final area of interests espouses the relevance of African American core texts for Historically Black Colleges and Universities. HBCUs are in a unique position to reframe the discussion of what constitutes a core text. Many of the works discussed within this context are works of the Ancient world, such as Homer's *Iliad* and *Odyssey* and Ovid's *Metamorphoses*, or the classic works of the modern world, such as *The Grapes of Wrath* and *Of Mice and Men* by Steinbeck and Tennessee Williams' *The Glass Menagerie*. Throughout history, these "great books" have shaped our culture and broadened our intellectual range. and have provided a framework from which to understand the complexities of human nature and thought. We embrace these compositions as a fundamental aspect of our literary heritage; however, a comprehensive understanding of our place in the world is incomplete without a broad-based discussion of the works that embody the African American cultures and traditions.

In introducing students to often forgotten "great works" by African American literary pioneers (such as *Clotel, Considered,* thought by many to be the first novel published by an African American, written by William Wells Brown; *The Marrow of Tradition,* a historical novel by Charles W. Chestnutt; and Jessie Redmon Fauset's *Plum Bun*) and to more contemporary readings (such as Richard Wright's *Native Son* and Ralph Ellison's *Invisible Man*), stirring characters such as Clotel, Bigger Thomas, and Angela Murray are able to provide a vibrant and provocative chronicle of African American life throughout history.

These works provide students with a far-reaching context in which to engage in critical self-assessment and also encourage them to examine fundamental questions about human nature, inclusive of African American culture and tradition.

Work Cited

McDowell, Deborah. "Introduction: Regulating Midwives." *Plum Bun: A Novel Without a Moral.* Boston: Beacon Press, 1990.

Silko's *Ceremony* as a Core Text: Natural and Unnatural Worlds

Jean-Marie Kauth
Benedictine University

> Then they grow away from the earth
> then they grow away from the sun
> then they grow away from the plants and animals.
> They see no life.
> When they look
> they see only objects.
> The world is a dead thing for them
> the trees and rivers are not alive
> the mountains and stones are not alive.
> The deer and bear are objects.
> They see no life.
>
> —Leslie Marmon Silko, *Ceremony* (135)

In talking about engaging worlds through core texts, we most often speak of worlds imagined, of worlds remembered, of the world abstracted in science, of the world occupied, manipulated, and recreated by people. If we see nature, it is nature fashioned to our liking, as Eden, as the *hortus inclusus*. Even in Thoreau and Wordsworth, where nature is encountered more or less wild and untamed, nature is still perceived as something outside of self, outside of the human. Or rather, the human is understood as outside of and to some degree in control of nature. Even the word *stewardship* implies that we are active agents over a passive and inert nature.

In a new environmental course that covered a great deal of ground, everything from Thoreau's *Walden* to Sandra Steingraber's *Living Downstream*, Leslie Marmon

Silko's *Ceremony* played a key role in the discussion of ecology and was successful in helping students understand a worldview in which humans are only a small part of a larger existence. Many of the texts in the course could best be described as science writing for a general audience; other pieces fell under the category of nature writing; this novel, while not directly alluding to environmental issues, provided one of the best bases for examining the cultural underpinnings of our attitudes towards the environment, in part because of the contrast between European and Native American (Laguna) poetry, metaphors, and stories. I would advocate for *Ceremony* as an excellent new core text in environmental literature, as well as in more general core courses. In keeping with the conference theme, *Ceremony* constructs a world for us—one often hidden from non-Native Americans—in which the ecological destructiveness of the twentieth century is played out and remediated. Reading it, students better understood the concept of Gaia and asked an important question: why does European culture see Nature as something outside of human nature?

In the quote with which I began, "they" view the earth as dead. In fact, my experience has very much fit with this description. How many of us would agree that we see rocks and rivers as dead, or at least inanimate, and animals and plants as objects? In the medieval great chain of being, humans were at least on a continuum with animals, plants, and even rocks. Now, we understand rocks as mineral wealth or inert molecules, chop down plants with little regard even for their life-giving oxygen production, and find our animals mostly neatly wrapped in plastic at the supermarket. Students speak of the environment as some *thing* that they can choose either to care for or not, without any sense of real consequences for themselves. This last part, the consequence of ecological devastation on themselves, is easily challenged with information like that available at the CDC Biomonitoring Project, which shows that even babies are now born contaminated with hundreds of different neurotoxic, carcinogenic, and estrogenic synthetic chemicals. Steingraber's *Living Downstream* provides another reality check. But countering the other part, the notion that they not only depend upon the environment, but *are* part of the environment, is much harder to convey. These are students with a pitifully tenuous connection to the Earth. They spend little time outdoors and rarely camp or hike. The few animals they see in suburbia, they tend to view with aversion. In our class alone, individuals professed hatred for deer, geese, and squirrels. They prefer animals as seen on TV, exotic, distant, and mediated through technology. They are part of the "last child in the woods" generation.[1] We talked a great deal about how we see the world, about art and nature and the combination of the two. On a cold, drizzly day while reading Thoreau, I took the students to the lake a hundred yards away and had them look carefully at *some thing*, see with Thoreau's eyes, and write for fifteen minutes about what they saw while they saw it. Though it was not enough to change a whole life of not seeing nature, the exercise produced some original insights and changed our whole conversation.

Ceremony paints a world in which plants, animals, humans, and the earth itself all play roles in each other's lives. Even rocks live in this worldview. The white belief that "the mountains and the stones are not alive," implies that the Laguna believe they are. We see the violation of the mountains in the yellow rocks that fuel an atomic bomb, a thing wholly unnatural, whose destruction the main character Tayo witnesses half a world away. We see the strength of living rock as Tayo begins to regain health, drinking water from a pool in which he can "taste the deep heartrock of the earth, where the water all came from" (46). Towards the end, healed perhaps from the trauma of his war experience, but lying badly hurt from a fall from his horse, Tayo feels his connection to the earth: "It was pulling him back, close to the earth, where the core was cool and silent as mountain stone, and...he knew how it would be: a returning rather than a separation.... He was sinking into the elemental arms of mountain silence" (201). The cool, living earth contrasts with the dead ash of the "witchery" and the slimy mud of the jungles in which Tayo fought.[2]

The world portrayed in *Ceremony* is very different from students' in the relationship to animals as well. Tayo remembers hunting a deer with his cousin Rocky. Newly dead, the dear is beautiful:

> He knelt and touched the nose: it was softer than pussy willows, and cattails, and still warm as a breath. The bright blood in the nostrils was still wet. He touched the big mule-size ears, and they were still warm, he knew it would not last long: the eyes would begin to cloud and turn glassy green, then gray, sinking back in the skull. The nose would harden, and the ears would get stiff. But for that moment it was so beautiful that he could only stand and feel the presence of the deer: he knew what they say about deer was true. (50–51)

What they say about deer is that the deer comes to die out of love. While Rocky rejects Laguna ways, Tayo covers the head of the deer with his jacket before gutting it, out of respect for the deer. His uncle sprinkles the deer with cornmeal to feed the deer's spirit and show appreciation for the deer's voluntary gift of itself. Once home, the family will lay it out on a blanket, sprinkle more cornmeal, and adorn it with turquoise and silver. Even those Laguna who are Catholic, who participate in white culture, preserve the rite of the deer. This is a world completely foreign, completely antithetical to the culture of *Food, Inc.* For the most part, we are so distanced from our food, that we not only rarely see our meat on the hoof, but we eat things that are reduced to component parts, mixed with non-food ingredients, reassembled in factories into unrecognizable food-like substances, packaged in plastic, and sold in supermarkets. As Michael Pollan says, we eat culture, not Nature.

The Laguna people exist in the same world as the whites, but they see and experience a very different world, a world in parallel that is nonetheless affected by the actions of the white invaders or the Laguna witches who haunt the story. The anger and wounding Tayo experiences during the war overlaps with the anger and self-loathing Native Americans experience watching as the land stolen from them is desecrated and destroyed. For the Laguna, the land does not belong to the people, but the people to the land. The world we encounter in *Ceremony* is not a world that has been created by a God made in man's image, and given to humans to use. Nature is already there, and complete, though thought and talked into reality by Thought-Woman and her sisters. But if humans play no role in creating Nature, they do create worlds through language, through stories.

At the same time that *Ceremony* challenges students' understanding of the physical world, it also shakes up their expectations for how the world is imagined in words and story. We spent most of a class period discussing a page upon which only one word appeared: "Sunrise" (4). We talked about conventional expectations for stories, blank space, the difficulty of representing nature, the reader's participation in creating the world of the novel, and the indescribable qualities of Nature that the blank space represents. The book is full of surprises; often, the narrative lapses into traditional chants and poem-like visions of the other world.[3] The book begins

> Thought-Woman, the spider,
> named things and
> as she named them they appeared.
> She is sitting in her room
> thinking of a story now
> I'm telling you the story she is thinking. (1)

So the world is made by naming, and the story we read is the making of a world. When Ku'oosh, the medicine man, first comes to speak with Tayo, he speaks Laguna, carefully explaining each word:

> The word he chose to express "fragile" was filled with the intricacies of a continuing process, and with a strength inherent in spider webs woven across paths. . . . It took a long time to explain the fragility and intricacy because no word exists alone, and the reason for choosing each word had to be explained with a story about why it must be said this certain way. That was the responsibility that went with being human, old Ku'oosh said, the story behind each word must be told so there could be no mistake in the meaning of what had been said. (35–36)

Just as the natural world is inextricably interconnected, so stories form an ecosystem of words, and the stories and the natural world are also interconnected. According to one of the interpolated tales, it was the story of an ancient Laguna witch that, once uttered, brought white men and the destruction they wrought upon the world.

The abuse of nature portrayed in *Ceremony* is seen as one with the abuse of fellow human beings in the novel. We find out that the sin that makes Tayo sick is that, slogging through the wet jungles of the Pacific, losing his beloved cousin to Japanese soldiers as the rain poured down, Tayo became "a man who cursed the rain clouds, a man of monstrous dreams" (39). Tayo thinks his curse has ruined his native landscape, left it to wither, but he finds that the injury done to Nature was perpetrated by many others. The war is portrayed as both a sin against nature and a sin against other humans, as whites commit unimaginable atrocities from a distance: "Ku'oosh would have looked at the dismembered corpses and the atomic heat-flash outlines, where human bodies had evaporated, and the old man would have said something close and terrible had killed these people. Not even oldtime witches killed like that" (37). The treatment of women under white culture is seen as equally unnatural and dehumanizing. To heal, Tayo forges a relationship with T'seh, who is both Laguna woman and spirit, represented as a pregnant she-elk "painted in pale lavender clay on the south face of the sandstone, along the base of the cliff rock" (230). Only in coming to love the Earth itself in bodily form does Tayo heal the wounds of war and alienation from Nature and his native tradition inflicted by the modern world.

At the end of the class, it was *Ceremony* that had best voiced what I hoped students would take away from the class. Wise old Ku'oosh tells Tayo, "But you know, grandson, this world is fragile" (35). "The world is fragile" became a keystone concept in the class, linking scientific evidence of the damage we have done to ourselves and the world, Aldo Leopold's description of devastated yet beautiful Sand County, and Thoreau's intricate vision of the many colors of ice on Walden Pond. The fact that the world is fragile—as are we—is a core learning outcome for students and for citizens at large that increases in importance with every passing year. Environmental literacy must become part of our culture of learning and our national conversation. *Ceremony* creates a world and a cultural context that very directly challenges the modern world in which we live, while at the same time reminding us of the importance and beauty of the natural world just outside our doors.

Notes

1. Shedd Aquarium in Chicago has begun catering to this generation by covering up the windows that look onto the lake, creating Disney-like movie characters that become the show, and projecting images of an actress interacting with the dolphins on the screen; attention is diverted almost completely away from the animals, already in an artificial environment, and directed toward their images on huge screens, along with lights, a boat that floats in from the rafters, and actors in penguin suits, bizarre fantasy costumes, and medieval garb. This is only one example of how nature is dressed up and distanced from children, chosen because the Shedd should know better. It replaces a more standard dolphin show filled with educational information about the animals.

2 See Paula Gunn Allen (*Sacred Hoop*) for a discussion of witchery and the delusion that humans can be separate from nature.

3. Silko was criticized for weaving secret chants and stories into *Ceremony*, a testament to its authenticity. See Allen (*Special Problems*) for a critique of Silko's revelation of secrets, but also Wolfgang Hochbruck, who argues that the tales are neither authentic nor particular to a single tribe.

Works Cited

Allen, Paula Gunn. *The Sacred Hoop: Recovering the Feminine in American Indian Traditions.* Boston: Beacon, 1986.

——. "Special Problems in Teaching Leslie Marmon Silko's Ceremony." *American Indian Quarterly* 23.4 (1990): 379–86.

Hochbruck, Wolfgang. 'I Have Spoken': Fictional 'Orality' in Indigenous Fiction. *College Literature* 23.2 (1996): 132–42.

Pollan, Michael. *The Omnivore's Dilemma: A Natural History of Four Meals.* New York: Penguin, 2007.

Silko, Leslie Marmon. *Ceremony.* New York: Penguin, 1988.

Part V. Political Worlds and Worldly Politics

Socrates and Crito: Anxiety and the Engagement between the Empirical and Analytic (Ideal) Worlds of Athens

Kieran Bonner
St. Jerome's University, University of Waterloo

"The *Crito*," states Harold Tarrant in his introduction to the Penguin edition, "is a short but highly controversial work" (73). Socrates' theory in relation to the need to obey his agreement with the Laws of Athens, he says, "is incredibly strained" (76), raising logical implications that would deconstruct Socrates' explanation for not escaping. Tarrant resolves this strain by stating, "it is not to Athenian intellectuals that Plato addresses himself, but to the many patriotic citizens who found Socrates' failure to escape difficult to explain" (77). That is, to draw on the conference theme, it is "the world and cultural context" of ancient Athens that help explain the "activities, actors, and agents constituted in this core text."

This is a common pedagogical response to the concerns that students can and do come up when being taught this core text. It is an answer that requires teachers to go outside the text to solve a textual problem. However, does this text offer possibilities of engaging the world of Athens in other than empirical fashion (that is, the cultural world of the ancients)? In what way might this dialogue provide a way to see an engagement between the empirical world of family, friends, and patriotic citizens of an empirical ancient Athens and a more analytic or ideal Athenian world that Socrates can be understood to be arguing from? This paper provides a reading of the *Crito* that introduces students to what an engagement with Athens as an ideal community could look like, an engagement that shows Socrates' assessment to operate in a particular cultural context but not be "subservient to it" (Gadamer, *Truth and Method* 35).

The scene of the dialogue is the prison of Socrates. Crito has come with the news that the ship from Delos is due into Athens the next day, meaning an imminent execution for Socrates. When Crito admits that he has been in the cell for some time, Socrates asks "why did you not wake me at once" (Crito 43b). Crito replies, "Indeed, Socrates. I wish that I myself were not so sleepless and sorrowful. But I have been wondering to see how soundly you sleep. And I purposely did not wake you, for I was anxious not to disturb your repose" (43b). Naming his own anxiety, Crito remarks that Socrates' life-long happy temperament still holds under the calamity that is happening, indicating the Socratic claim that happiness, justice, and wisdom are inter-related. Is Socrates happy, despite the imminent prospect of his execution, because he has acted well and continues to act well in the situation of his trial and condemnation?

Crito, on the other hand, is sleepless and sorrowful. Why? One of his very good friends is about to die; the friend, who is a model of self-reflection and just action, is about to be executed because he has absurdly and unjustly been given the death penalty for impiety. Socrates death is a "double disaster," Crito says, since he will not only lose an irreplaceable friend, but he also risks being castigated as a poor friend: "and what reputation could be more disgraceful than the reputation of caring more for money than for one's friends. The public will never believe that we were anxious to save you, but that you yourself refused to escape" (44b–44c).

Crito offers a strong case for why Socrates not only *should* escape, but also why he *must* escape: "I think you will be doing what is unjust if you abandon your life when you might preserve it," he says (45c). Socrates, by abandoning his children, will be abandoning his parental obligations and bringing disgrace on all his friends who now will look like cowards who are more concerned with saving themselves than with risking action to save their friend. "Take care, Socrates," Crito says, "lest these things be not evil only, but also dishonorable to you and to us. Reflect, then, or rather the time for reflection is past: we must make up our minds" (46a).

Two things happen here. Crito charges Socrates with being in danger of acting unjustly if he refuses to escape. Second, we see that Crito's anxiety is becoming dominant, so dominant that he takes back the call for reflection: "if we delay any longer," he says, "we are lost" (46a). And reflection is time consuming. So one issue for this dialogue is how we handle our anxieties and fears about evil things that will happen to us (death, or the loss of a friend, or the loss of a good reputation); what does a good friend (and, by implication, a good Athenian) do with this anxiety? Is Socrates so self content that he is asleep to the catastrophic consequences that his actions will have on his friends?

Socrates acknowledges Crito's anxiety: "My dear Crito, if your anxiety to save me be right, it is most valuable" (46b). That is, Crito's anxiety, in itself, is not a bad thing, which affirms Gadamer's claim that "anxiety concerning existence is something which belongs inseparably to the life and nature of human beings" (*Enigma of Health* 158). For Socrates, we should be anxious about doing the right thing. However, he says, we need to avoid letting our anxiety control our relation to doing what is right. Doing what is right in this case requires getting some distance on our fears and terrors. Socrates describes his way of getting this distance: "I am still what

I have always been—a man who will accept no argument but that which on reflection I find to be the truest" (46b). If Socrates' commitment to theorizing was tested in his public trial by the threat of the prosecutor and jury (Blum, 175–217), then it is tested here by the potentially justified anxiety of his good friend. Unlike the threat of the multitude, this concern of Crito's, in fact, makes Socrates anxious: "I am anxious, Crito, to examine our former argument with your help, and to see whether my present circumstance will appear to me to have affected its truth in any way or not; and whether we are to set it aside, or to yield assent to it" (46d). So, we now have two people who are anxious, both anxious about whether the action, Socrates accepting his death sentence, is right or not.

Does this help us understand something about the relationship between anxiety and friendship? When a good friend is anxious about a future loss (friendship, reputation)—a loss that raises ethical concerns—he or she might try to work through the issue, to engage, that is, in radical reflection to see whether their anxiety is based on a truth or on a natural if "childish" fear that needs to be resisted. Not all fears and terrors point to actions that need to be avoided. Some fears are misleading, bringing out the child in us, tempting us to run rather than face the object of our fear courageously. Socrates points to a productive anxiety—not avoiding what we fear (death) but avoiding doing something wrong. Socrates has become anxious and now asks for his friend's help in understanding whether accepting his unjust sentence is ethical. For Socrates, handling this anxiety requires reflection. As his friend, Crito agrees.

The conversation among friends is the Socratic way to address the anxiety about whether the action one is about to undertake is ethical. The phenomenon of death itself has now been made incidental. It will be left to the *Phaedo* for us to get an image of what a confrontation with this phenomenon looks like. The reputation of Socrates or of Socrates' friends is also rendered incidental to the need to get Crito's help in resolving this current anxiety. Could we say that the interaction between Crito and Socrates has now turned into a genuine engagement? Socrates seems to be coming from a world that prevents him from agreeing with Crito's argument, despite the fact that "the anxiety concerning death...is part of the fundamental disposition of human beings" (Gadamer, *Enigma of Health* 155). It seems Socrates' reflective conversation with Crito enables Crito to get distance on the anxious rejection of reflection.

Crito agrees to Socrates' proposal that "living well and honorably and justly mean the same thing" (48b)—an agreement and knowledge that come from being influenced by a Socratic orientation. There are many examples of dialogues where the understanding that virtue, honor, justice, and happiness are deeply intertwined would be challenged (e.g., Polus and Callicles in the *Gorgias* and Thrasymachus in the *Republic*). However, here we have a conversation between Socrates and his friend, Crito, a conversation that can take for granted the argument needed to establish the principle that it is better to suffer an injustice than do an injustice. It is on the basis of the influence of friendship that Socrates says, "we have nothing to consider but the question...shall we be acting justly if we give money and thanks to the men who are to aid me in escaping and if we ourselves take our respective parts in my escape?" (48c–48d). Where in our contemporary era the whole issue of assisted suicide opens an ethical Pandora's box, here it is assisted living that raises the ethical concern. It is at this point that Crito agrees to set aside issues around "considerations of expense, and of reputation, and of bringing up my children, of which you talk, Crito" as the opinions of the multitude (48c). As Socrates seeks to relieve his own anxiety about the ethicality of his action, he has helped Crito get some distance on his anxiety about the potential damage to his reputation as a friend that Socrates' actions put at risk. The friendly conversation enables Crito to override the anxiety about his reputation as a friend and say, "I think you are right, Socrates. But what are we to do?" (48d).

Crito is now anxious about what Socrates is anxious about (is it ethical or just to escape?) but is unsure about how to go about resolving this question. The "what are we to do" question suggests that Socrates has induced an *aporia*, whose urgency has now replaced his previous anxiety about his reputation as a friend. At this point, Socrates becomes very direct in his conversation with Crito: "Let us examine this question together, my friend, and if you can contradict anything that I say, do so, and I shall be persuaded...I am very anxious to act with your approval and consent. I do not want you to think me mistaken" (48e). Socrates was sleeping soundly, but now, awakened to his friend's disapproval of his actions, he has become very anxious. So, while the anxiety concerning the reputation of being a friend has been displaced in this conversation, the approval of an actual friend, in and through this very conversation, has become very urgent.

When Socrates asks Crito, "if I escape without the state's consent...shall I be abiding by my just agreements or not," Crito replies: "I cannot answer your question, Socrates. I do not understand it" (49e–50a). Is there something about Crito's understanding of his friendship with Socrates that makes it difficult for him to understand the insight that keeps Socrates from escaping from prison? Is there a way Socrates can make available a world that can ground his insight and make his refusal to escape seem less eccentric? To help with this problem in understanding, Socrates imagines the laws and the commonwealth interrogating him as if he was "preparing to run away" (50a). That is, Socrates constructs a world where he has to defend himself from the charge that to escape would be to respond unjustly to what he is unjustly suffering.

In essence, Socrates has the Athenian Commonwealth argue that by escaping, Socrates' action could be interpreted in such a way that it could be seen to threaten the fabric of Athenian social life and the integrity of his own life as a defender of laws (Cumming xii–xiii). While this remains a reasonable position, it can nevertheless be argued that by his actions Socrates did in fact put the fabric of Athenian social life at risk. Also, there is no way to ensure that Socrates' actions, whether escaping or not escaping, will not be interpreted as damaging to Athens. As stated above, according to Tarrant, Socrates' theory here is "incredibly strained" (76). "Supposing Socrates was innocent of the charges brought by Meletus," Tarrant says, "was he not guilty of bringing the law into disrepute by allowing himself to be convicted and put to death? . . . If injustice is the greatest of evils for the person who commits it, then the son who cherishes his parent ought to do his utmost to avoid having that parent be unjust to him" (75–76). For these reasons, Tarrant resolves these logical dilemmas by resorting to empirical knowledge about Crito—"a follower of Socrates, owing some loyalty to Socratic moral principles but perhaps no great intellectual" (77)—and to the cultural context of ancient Athens—"it is not to Athenian intellectuals that Plato addresses himself, but to the many patriotic citizens who found Socrates' failure to escape difficult to accept" (77).

However, we now recognize that this particular resort to the cultural context argument leaves out the issue of friendship, of being concerned for the damage to a friend's reputation. It also avoids both the question of how to resolve the anxiety about doing the right thing and the place of reflexive theorizing in coming to an understanding of just action. Why does Crito, who finds Socrates happy and sleeping well, arouse so much anxiety in Socrates? How is one, who is "perhaps no great intellectual," able to disturb Socrates' slumbering contentment?[1] In this case, we must ask, how does the Athenian Commonwealth conduct itself in the dialogue? What particular kinds of questions animate this interlocutor?

In its argument with Socrates, the Athenian Commonwealth argues that he must respect his parents as those who make the gift of life possible. But Socrates goes on to have the Commonwealth say:

> Socrates, we have very strong evidence that you were satisfied with us and with the state. You would not have been content to stay at home in it more than other Athenians unless you had been satisfied with it more than they...Are we right, or are we wrong, in saying that you have agreed not in mere words, but in your actions to live under our government? (52b–52d).

What Socrates has the Athenian Commonwealth say is: Socrates, this is the life you have lived and this way of living is grounded in implicit agreements. In fact, this is true of all of our everyday actions. Harold Garfinkel, in a variety of "experiments," showed the pervasiveness with which "persons will hold each other to agreements whose terms they never actually stipulated" (73).[2] In a sense, the Laws of Athens are calling Socrates' attention to this *et cetera clause*, the implied agreement embedded in action. That is, Socrates generates a community (called the Athenian Commonwealth) who call attention to the implicit agreement (though the terms were "never actually stipulated") that his life of examination rests upon.

Socrates' friendship with the city enabled him to make significant life questions come to life through conversation. Just as his friendship with Crito (and this very dialogue that is the embodiment of that friendship) provides Socrates with the basis for resolving anxiety about acting justly in this occasion, so too did his friendship with Athens provide Socrates with the cultural context that made the examined life possible. If Socrates is the "man who will accept no argument but that which on reflection [he] finds to be the truest" (46b), then Athens is the kind of city that made the examined life both possible and enjoyable. Up to and including his last days, Athens provided Socrates with the cultural context to develop into the man he had to be: the man who came to understand the intricate interrelation between the examined life, the just life, and the happy life. In this reading, the Athenian Commonwealth is Socrates' way of generating an image of an authoritative community, a community that values the principles that Socrates aims to embody in action. As such, the Commonwealth's position is Socrates' way of making alive to Crito an engagement with a world that ground Socrates' actions. The Athenian Commonwealth becomes Socrates' reflexive reminder that Athens was both the context in which he worked through the demand to live an examined life and a particular context that made the working out of that demand enjoyable. Socrates sleeps soundly because he knows that the necessary life of reflection was also an enjoyable life of examination.

In this sense, Socrates points to the intimate connection between a sense of community and a sense of taste. Taste, says Gadamer, has a normative power, "which is peculiar to it alone, the knowledge that it is certain of the agreement of an ideal community…We see here the ideality of good taste…Taste makes an act of knowledge, in a manner which it is true cannot be separated from the concrete situation on which it operates and cannot be reduced to rules and concepts" (*Truth and Method* 36). Socrates loves the city that made what he needed to do—live an examined life—an enjoyable project. The Athenian Commonwealth is Socrates' way of reminding himself and Crito of the kind of world the theorist needs to engage in order to ground an action and a life (McHugh 1–20).

Notes

A longer, different version of this paper was published as Kieran Bonner, "Principles, dialectic and the common world of friendship: Socrates and Crito in conversation." *History of the Human Sciences* 27.2 (April 2014): 3–25.

1. Perhaps the concern with reputation that worries Crito need not be so much at the hands of fellow Athenians as at the hands of British professors of ancient philosophy and classics?

2. Garfinkel calls this pervasive feature of everyday life "a method for discovering agreements by eliciting or imposing a respect for the rule of practical circumstances" (74) and he illustrates it with the experiment "in which the experimenter engaged others in conversation while he had a wire recorder hidden under his coat. In the course of the conversation the experimenter opened his jacket to reveal the recorder saying, 'See what I have?' An initial pause was almost invariably followed by the question, 'what are you going to do with it?'… An agreed privacy was thereupon treated as though it had operated all along" (75). Garfinkel calls this a method of discovering agreements articulating an *et cetera clause.*

Works Cited

Blum, Alan. *Socrates: The Original and Its Images*. London: Routledge and Kegan Paul, 1978.

Cumming, Robert. *Introduction*. Plato. *Euthyphro, Apology & Crito*. New York: Macmillan Publishing Company, 1956. vii–xv.

Gadamer, Hans Georg. *Truth and Method*. London: Sheed and Ward, 1975.

———. *The Enigma of Health: The Art of Healing in a Scientific Age*. Trans. Jason Gaiger and Nicholas Walker. Stanford: Stanford UP, 1996.

Garfinkel, Harold. *Studies in Ethnomethodology*. Cambridge: Polity Press, 1967.

McHugh, P. et al. *On the Beginning of Social Inquiry*. London: Routledge and Kegan Paul, 1974.

Plato. *Euthyphro, Apology & Crito*. Trans. F. J. Church. Trans. rev. Robert Cumming. New York: Macmillan Publishing Company, 1956.

Tarrant, Harold. *Introduction*. Plato. *The Last Days of Socrates: Euthyphro, Apology, Crito, Phaedo*. London: Penguin Books, 2003. ix–xxxi.

Economics as a Force of Nature in Aristotle's *Politics*: An Antireductionist View

Molly Brigid Flynn
Assumption College

THE PROBLEM OF ECONOMICS IN POLITICS

As Richard Mulgan emphasizes, "Aristotle believes the political conflicts of his day are principally due to a clash between two economic groups, the rich and the poor, who support two different types of constitution (oligarchy and democracy) with different political principles (wealth and freedom)" (64). Yes. According to Aristotle, the rich regularly hold oligarchic positions, the poor democratic positions, and their factions despise each other. The extreme result of their contest is a degradation of politics to a fight for power littered with sloganized rationalizations. It is tempting to psychoanalyze these justifications away cynically or skeptically, claiming that politics is really about power or that economics completely determines one's political views. The economic influence on political opinions threatens the reasonableness of politics and inspires economic reductionist theories of it. To confidently reject such reductions, we need a better explanation of the economic influence in politics. Aristotle offers one.

But Mulgan implies that Aristotle's analysis is stuck in his time, in his culture, in his economic and political context. Aristotle presents economic bias and difference as sub-political, permanent features of human politics. The *Politics* is not just an historical text, but something that speaks to our students directly by making claims about human nature and the way we tend to form political opinions. It also forces us to appreciate a profound political need: civic virtue must address economic differences wisely to safeguard a healthy politics and our good life together.

THE FORCE OF ECONOMICS IN POLITICS

Since economic difference wreaks havoc on politics, perhaps we should just level property. Leveling could be done only by the expropriation typical of extreme democracies, and Aristotle condemns it as unjust and destructive of the city. Moreover, it would not eliminate factional conflict.

> For the property of the citizens to be equal. then. is indeed an advantage with a view to avoiding factional conflict between them. but by no means a great one. ... For the nature of desire is without limit. and it is with a view to satisfying this that the many live. (69; II.7.1267a)

For Aristotle, economics is not the essentially responsible factor behind the factional split between the wealthy and the poor; the more fundamental cause is their characters. judgments about what they deserve, and desires for what they imagine they can get. Aristotle remarks, "one ought to level desires sooner than property" (68; II.7.1266b) and recommends moral education as more important than adjusting the distribution of property. But if character matters more than money, how should we read Aristotle's economically focused analysis of regimes and factions?

A man's opinions. not his economic identity. determines whether he advocates a certain regime. Wealth and poverty are sub-political features of factioners, seemingly incidental to their political characters and to the nature of their regimes. Yet wealth and poverty are the psychological motors behind oligarchic and democratic constitutions because they powerfully contribute to a man's character and thus his opinions about justice and the common good.

One's view of the *telos* of human life is. according to Aristotle. the primary determinant of one's political principles, and extreme economic conditions of one's upbringing strongly distort one's view of the good life. The rich tend to identify wealth as the good life, and thus the city's *telos*, and so espouse oligarchic "justice" and policies to maintain their wealth and privilege. The poor tend to identify living as one pleases as the good life. and so see freedom as the city's *telos*, and thus espouse democratic "justice" and policies such as redistribution that help each more easily and equally live as he pleases.

So for Aristotle the defining principles of oligarchy and democracy are the views of justice espoused—equality for the poor and superiority for the rich—and their views are partially correct: "The cause of this is that the judgment concerns themselves, and most people are bad judges concerning their own things" (97; III.9.1280a). Aristotle points out that people's political principles tend to be influenced by their economic situations, simply because one's self-interest in a policy skews the appearance of its justice.

But more deeply, living the rich or poor life distorts one's emotional habits, one's understanding of the good human life, and ultimately one's views of justice and the common good. The practical reason of the rich and the poor is governed by emotional undercurrents (arrogance and contempt. envy and malice) that distort their relationships with whoever appears as their opposite in possessions. One result is that they view the city not as a partnership but as a contest. Another is that they are incapable of properly ruling or being ruled. As Aristotle points out, many extreme conditions have this effect, though wealth and poverty are the most politically significant. When it comes to the goods of fortune, the very lucky "tend to become arrogant and base on a grand scale," while the very unlucky become "malicious and base in petty ways." Even "from the time they are children at home," such people can neither rule nor be ruled well, humanely, maturely. "So the ones do not know how to rule but only to be ruled, and then only in a fashion of rule of a master, and the others do not know how to be ruled by any sort of rule, but only to rule in the fashion of rule of a master. What comes into being, then, is a city not of free persons but of slaves and masters, the ones consumed by envy, the others by contempt" (134; IV.11.1295b).

Aristotle discussed masterly rule when he described the relationships within the household, the original economic unit. As pre-political, genetic parts of the city, households and villages remain in the city, and the relationships forged there continue to have force in the city's life. The sub-political economic dealings between rich and poor people shape them as political actors, because their characters take on an emotional impetus that plays out politically. The city informed by a good and just constitution is the fulfillment of these human groups, but material is not always fully governed by its form. This is so especially when forming the material requires discernment and decision, as it does in human action. That the rich and the poor are the primary factional parts of the city indicates that, according to Aristotle, the politics of most cities fails to achieve a truly political level because the usual regime-forming actors are dominated by sub-political styles of rule.

There are certainly among the poor and rich those who are not vicious in their political views, who may not fully believe the exclusivist slogans of their factions. Like the more or less incontinent man whose emotions can overthrow his better judgment, the poor and the rich can be radicalized into acting as Aristotle's stereotypes of democrats and oligarchs. The emotions that especially bias their vision of justice are, for the rich, contempt, arrogance, and fear of the many, and for the poor, envy, malice, and fear of the rich. Furthermore, as one faction is aroused (we call this, exciting the base), these emotions are more evoked in the other, such that factions reciprocally reinforce each other's emotional vulnerabilities. Given the snowballing effect of factional hatred and fear in a city, we can understand how the situation Aristotle describes could arise in which the factioners openly pronounce their hatred and vow to fight, scatter, and destroy each other.

One's economic situation does not directly or necessarily determine one's view of justice: it just happens that being embedded in certain *extreme* economic situations distorts one's views. Aristotle claims both the virtuous and those in the economic middle escape having their perceptions of justice twisted by economic extremes. The virtuous are too few to have much of an effect on factions in a city (154; V.4.1304b), but the middle can be a quantitatively significant group and are more open to virtue than are the rich or the poor.

The middle is free of the economic extremes that most powerfully distort one's understanding of the good human life, the common good, and justice; just as importantly, they are not pulled into the political polarization because they neither plot against, nor are plotted against by, economic enemies. The middle avoids the emotions that badly bias oligarchs' and democrats' opinions about justice—this avoidance and the fact that the middle can be friends with both the wealthy and the poor explain their ability to ground a good regime by allowing it to overcome the distrust that destroys friendship. The middle does not have exhaustive or philosophical knowledge of justice. They are not even on the whole virtuous. Their perception of justice may be distorted by other personal malformed dispositions, but it is undistorted by the economic extremes that especially undermine political friendship. This gives them a vital role to play in Aristotle's good regimes. Only a city with a strong middling element is capable of avoiding the destructive domination of factions.

ECONOMICS AND THE BODY POLITIC: PERSONAL, ANIMAL, OR VEGETABLE?

Aristotle says that he will investigate the city by looking at its parts. The city is a complex thing, having many parts and many types of parts. In Book I, the analytic method focuses Aristotle's attention on the *genetic* parts of the city—he is interesting in displaying what the city is by showing "how things develop naturally from the beginning" (35; I.2.1252a). He then discusses the household, its members, the types of rule found within it, and its natural outgrowth, the village. From the union of villages, a city arises, and in it, these genetic parts are surpassed by the community capable of providing not just for continued life of the race but for a good human life. The many households and villages are not the rungs on a ladder thrown away when transcended; they constitute the embryonic material that remains in the city as a sub-political bodily substrate. Aristotle begins Book III by again saying that we must investigate the city by investigating its parts. Here he is focused on the persons who, through deliberations and decisions based on their various convictions about justice and the common good, shape the agglomeration of families and villages *politically*. From Book III's formal focus, the citizens are the primary parts, because a citizen is someone who shares in the regime.

In Books IV and V, Aristotle presents the rich and poor as the crucial parts of the city. But what kind of part? The rich and poor seem to be both genetic and formal. They are regime-forming caucuses of would-be rulers, determining the city's form when they gain power and articulate views of justice and the common good to validate their actions; yet they are groups, associated with clusters of households, distinguished by the pre-political differences of wealth and poverty and motivated by sub-political emotions and desires.

The constitution is supposed to be the form of the city analogous to the soul of an animal. Repeatedly Aristotle uses this analogy. Animals differ according to the arrangement of their parts, which determines how they seek sustenance, which determines their ways of life. Analogously, the many parts of the city yield different constitutions when arranged differently, seeking different goods as the end of the city, and the constitution "is the way of life of a city" (133; IV.11.1295a40). What an interesting animal the city is that by decision gives itself its soul and its way of life! Animal bodies are gradually informed, their parts made and arranged by nature operating on the embryonic material through the species-form of the father. Not so the city.

Seemingly, the better analogy for the city would be to the human person, whose nature requires a non-naturally growing complement, virtue. Virtue is natural, since it perfects us (*Physics* VII.3.246a-b), but it is not *native*. It doesn't develop non-deliberately by the workings of nature. Our emotional dispositions must be established by action, and must be worked upon by reason to become virtuous. A mass of villages may merely grow, but a regime involves reason. For a city to reach a good constitution, its parts must be subsumed into the whole, arranged justly, and ordered to the common good, just as the morally virtuous man establishes his character by taming and harnessing his desires in the activities of his good life.

But in explaining the city, Aristotle prefers the analogy to the body of brutes. Perhaps this is because in arranging its parts, this strange animal usually does not do so well, but puts its stomach-driven imagination in charge.

Various bodies of animals require hunting different food, and "differences in sustenance have made the ways of life of animals differ" (44; I.8.1256a). Likewise, seeking happiness defines the constitution and the city's way of life. "For it is through hunting for this [happiness] in a different manner and by means of different things that [groups of] individuals create ways of life and regimes that differ" (209; VII.8.1328a–b). The ultimate task of politics is to do this well, shaping the goals, rules, and habits of the people to allow and encourage the citizens to live good human lives. Because the good human life is not defined by material goods, politics at its core is not about economics. Economics appears in the *Politics* primarily as a sub-political reality that as a psychological force over regime-builders and trouble-makers is responsible for their *deformation* of the city.

After the *Politics'* study of factions, another biological analogy suggests itself. In *On the Soul*, Aristotle critiques Empedocles's reductionist theory of plant life. "Empedocles has not spoken well" in stating that "growth happens to plants when they take root downward because earth moves that way by nature, and when they spread upward because fire moves that way." He asks of Empedocles, "what is it that holds the fire and earth together when they move in opposite directions?" Were fire and earth not potential parts but fully active in the plant's body, they would continually go up and down, pulling the plant asunder. "For they will be torn apart if there is not something that prevents it, and if there is, this is the soul, and it is responsible for the growing and the feeding." In order to be parts of the stable unity of the plant, fire and earth must be combined into organs by the form, which limits and harnesses the elemental motion. "For the growth of fire goes on without limit, as long as there is something burnable, but all things put together by nature have a limit and proportion of size and growth, and this belongs to the soul" (*On the Soul* 92–93; II.4.415b33–416a18). The city as ruled by factions resembles Empedocles' plant, since the rich and the poor are material parts unwilling to be limited by a proper constitution. Imagining the goods they contribute to the city, wealth and freedom, to be the point of the city rather than instruments for the city's good life, they do not recognize limits on these goods or on their titles to rule. Like fire, desire is without limit. When they are radicalized and fully get their way, these groups tear the city asunder. The rich ruling most oligarchically or the poor most democratically is a tyranny and practically not a constitution at all—the whole can be held together only by violence.

The rich and poor are the primary factional parts of the city. Understanding the significance of this fact requires recognizing them as both material genetic parts and formal end-determining parts. Though antireductionist, Aristotle's account of economics in politics still requires us to recognize sub-political economic forces as a powerful political fact, and warns us that Empedocles' plant describes us at our worst.

Relative wealth and poverty are permanent features of human life, but it is exorbitant wealth and real poverty and an empty gap in between that give rise to profound factional conflict. Aristotle's responses to the economic causes of faction are recommendations aimed at moderating wealth and poverty, limiting the power of the rich and poor to abuse each other, and cultivating the economic middle.

To solve the threat of factions to a city, it is not enough to attend only to their ideological mistakes. Just as factionalism results largely from bad economic arrangements, political friendship has material prerequisites. Good regimes must be built on and foster a healthy body, a material substrate that allows the rich and poor to recognize one another as political friends.

Works Cited

Aristotle. *The Politics*. Trans. Carnes Lord. Chicago, IL: U of Chicago P, 1984.
————. *On the Soul*. Trans. Joe Sachs. Santa Fe, NM: Green Lion Press, 2001.
Mulgan, Richard. *Aristotle's Political Theory: An Introduction for Students of Political Theory*. Oxford: Clarendon Press, 1977.

Humanities Education and the Hidden Civic Virtue of Doubt

Mark Blackell
Vancouver Island University

The teaching of an integrated core curriculum involves, of course, exploring many different and fundamental questions. One recurring question is: What ought to unify people in a political community? Much of the western tradition has attempted to frame an answer to this question in terms of love and, in reading that tradition, a student can find herself simultaneously confronting her own preformed views on the political bond. For the sake of argument, and in keeping with my sense of the default mode of most students I encounter, I will imagine a student coming from a liberal in-dividualist perspective and reading two very different accounts of the role of love in political community. Most students I meet tend to assume that political community is a sort of a contract of autonomous individuals. When reading social contract theories of the rational interested nature of the political bond, students often see it as stating the obvious. Sometimes, and with some theories, students react to the atomism of the state of nature prior to a social contract, but they rarely, at least at first, object to the idea that political bond is rooted in rational self-interest by autonomous, contracting individuals.

Let's imagine such a student coming to the reading first of Dante's *Divine Comedy*, a poem that gives her a radically different account of the role of love in community. I find that one of the challenges for students encountering the *Inferno* for the first time is to understand the logic of the structure of hell and of why it is that those who commit treachery are furthest down in hell. Key to the reader's understanding is Virgil's explanation in Canto 11 where he explains to Dante-the-Pilgrim the distinctions between upper and lower hell in terms of love. The sins of incontinence, which "offend God least," involve a love that is misdirected, through some incontinence, to lower goods. The sins of fraud or malice that lie below the walls of the city of Dis are described as coming in two forms. Some, like hypocrisy, flattery, theft, simony, etc... involve a deception or fraud against one's neighbours that does a kind of violence to the social bond. Virgil claims that the simple malice in the next-to-lowest sphere "seems only to destroy the bond of love that Nature gives to man" (*Inferno* 11. 55–6). The lower form of malice or treachery against family members, kinsmen, and lords also "disregards the love Nature enjoys"; however, it goes further in violating what Virgil calls "that extra bond between men which creates a special trust" (*Inferno* 11. 61–3).

This latter idea of violating implicit forms of trust, as one finds in the family, or explicit trust that has been expressed in an oath is usually not that hard for students to understand. What they have trouble with is the more general idea that malice or fraud is most essentially a violation of the "bond of love that Nature gives to man." Why should flattery violate a bond of love? Why should hypocrisy or seduction be so low, even below a murderous rage that is a form of incontinence? Why do these sins violate a bond of love that is *natural*? The problem, of course, is that for our student to understand the logic of hell she needs to momentarily stop thinking about the essential nature of the bond of society as an interest-based contract to a natural order that expresses love. She also needs to think about love as not simply something that is merely a sentiment that a person possesses or a state of mind; she needs to stop thinking about love as merely subjective. Love, or *amor*, is indeed something personal in Dante's poem. Love begins with the love of the particular—just as Dante-the-Pilgrim's journey begins with his love of Beatrice as the animating force that allows him to gain the courage to enter hell. But love is also that which binds human community in its smaller units and its larger political entities. In Canto 17 of *Purgatory* we learn from Virgil of the distinction between a "natural love" that is the tendency of all things to seek the "primal good" without error and a "rational" or unnatural love that can err by loving the wrong object or loving the right object too little or too much. The essence of love, or "natural love," animates the properly used human will to move towards God. The personal, the political, and the metaphysical are united through this "Natural love."

This is a profoundly distinct vision from most students' initial understanding of love as a feeling or subjective state. As the students read about the sins of malice and think about how they are sins that undermine the means by which people know each other and exchange with each other, it becomes easier to see how reciprocity is undermined. At some point the student will hopefully see the possibility of the essential bond of community on a different model. I've never met a student who simply accepted a natural hierarchy of society, but I have met ones who began to think anew about the idea of love as a potential model of the bond of society. It occurs to me that while I want the student to decide for herself if she will accept such a different vision of the bond of community than she holds, I would not be happy with an adequate understanding coupled with an expression of absolute disinterest. I want the student to grapple with her own preformed views about what unifies community by thinking deeply about a very different vision. I want her, in other words, to be open to the possibility of doubting her own deeply held (if previously unformulated) view, even if she ends up reaffirming it in a more self-conscious fashion in the end. If I want this, however, am I saying that I think there is some virtue in doubt that is built into the education I seek?

If this openness to doubt about closely held beliefs is something I seek, why do I seek it in the texts we read? My sense is that the capacity of a given text to resist an indifferent intellectual grasp, and to generate doubt in the contemporary reader, has something to do with its artistic or philosophical depth. This is perhaps something that the idea of greatness in the term "great books program" is implicitly trying to get at. In the *Inferno*, the way to this more profound understanding of what is being said about love is through the poetic images. The power of the presentation of ideas lies not so much in Virgil's words, important as these are for the conceptual framework, as it does in the poetic account of the inherent horror of the nature of the sins. Our student may begin to think anew, if she is reading in an open way, about what it is to seduce or to flatter, or to be hypocritical; she begins to think, through the images and language of the poem, about what one does when one commits such acts. It helps to think anew about suicide as a suffering of incontinent self-expression, for example, when one is confronted with the images of Pier della Vigne embodied in a dead tree, having a limb broken "so from that splintered trunk a mixture poured/ of words and blood" (*Inferno* 13. 43–4). It helps to think about the nature of act of flattery, when the flatterer is represented as rolling around in excrement; the nature of the act itself is poetically represented. In part I think the moment of doubt is made possible because the student has had to work hard to get to that point of understanding by working her way through the poetic images and her initial reactions to them. The potential for the text to generate doubt is here inseparable from poetic form.

Let me now fast-forward in a chronological curriculum and think about our student reading Hannah Arendt's *The Human Condition*. Arendt presents our student with a very different take on the question of what ought to unite political community; for Arendt it *ought not* to be love. Arendt argues that modernity has tended to erode what she calls worldliness by being focussed on political life as the administration of things or on a model of politics as a form of engineering. She seeks to resuscitate the Ancient Greek concern with a phenomenological experience of what she calls action or the seeking of excellence in word and deed in a space of appearance before others. The Christian focus on love as a model for political community is one part of the larger problem of the loss of the space of appearances between people or of "worldliness." For Arendt,

> Love, by virtue of its passion, destroys the in-between which relates us to and separates us from others. . . . Love, by its very nature, is unworldly, and it is for this reason rather than its rarity that it is not only apolitical but antipolitical, perhaps the most powerful of all antipolitical human forces. (242)

Passionate love and spiritual love that unites one with the divine each seek their own versions of intimate unity, and, as such, they each erode the space between people that is the hallmark of human political life. Arendt contrasts the Christian concern with love, which drives forgiveness, with respect, which is a kind of friendship, and which is a form of uniting individuals in terms not of an intimate revelation of who they are so much as in terms of their qualities, achievements, and failings. Respect is more important than love because it allows for a disclosure of the self that is not intimate; it allows for the possibility of new beginnings as people respond to an actor's words and deeds not as personal, nor as part of a natural whole expressed in love, but as part of a shared political creation—as an artifice.

Our imaginary student is presented with an implicit objection to love as the bond of political community that she encountered in Dante. For love in *The Divine Comedy* is not only that which passionately unites Dante with Beatrice, but also unifies political community and moves the believer towards God. It unifies with profound spiritual intimacy, and it is precisely this intimacy that Arendt thinks erodes the distinct space of human political freedom. While "Natural love" for Dante is the basis of the human's relationship with God, the glue of the good political community, and the essence of true passionate love, political friendship for Arendt is distinct from passionate love on the one hand and divine love on the other.

If our student has her newfound appreciation for Dante's model thrown into doubt, Arendt does not provide a justification for a contractual, interest-based model that acted as our imaginary student's starting point. Arendt sees the power that emerges in collective action as unifying, but she doesn't see power as merely an expression of interest, nor does she see the political community that acts together out of respect to be simply a means to the end of individual gain. Our collective action is more in the service of human creativity than anything else. If the students take Arendt's argument seriously, she will need to also work hard at trying to understand the shift in perspective Arendt seeks in her reader. Arendt implicitly asks of her readers that they think about a fragile intersubjective world that is the space of political community and human freedom. On the same fundamental question our student is presented with another opportunity for doubt, and in this case it is less because of the power of the language (although this is part of it) than because of the depth of Arendt's account of a phenomenon that is threatened in modernity. Arendt presents us with a serious and deep concern about modernity whether or not we end up agreeing with her assessment.

So where does this leave our student? Clearly we would not be happy with mere doubt as the end-point for the student; I personally would want her to develop a position of the conversation she has been having with Dante, Arendt, and other thinkers. But, more important than what she concludes in response to the question about what the bond of political community ought to be is the fact that the thoughtful engagement with these ideas, coupled with doubt, may foster her capacity for doubt in the future.

Contemporary deliberative models of democracy see the core of democracy not in the process of expressing and collecting individual wills (as in an aggregative model of democracy) but in the deliberative process of the formation of wills *prior to their expression*. Much of deliberative democracy focuses on the communicative competence of citizens and on the access to information and the giving of informed meaningful reasons for political decisions. Deliberative democracy depends upon the idea that for a citizenry to move towards *truer* and *more* just decisions, individual citizens must be able to change their minds. From the point of view of deliberative democracy, the doubt made possible by deep reading of texts that present profound responses to fundamental questions is of inherent value in that it fosters the capacity for doubt in the future. Doubt is a democratic virtue, but it is a hidden virtue in that much of the Western tradition we examine has seen it in terms of a scepticism that has its role merely in terms of the way in which it leads to a philosophical or spiritual ascent. In such a view, doubt is a vital *stage* of intellectual development, but it is not constitutive of the end point. For a deliberative model of democracy doubt has a more *constitutive role* in that the process of deliberation, and thus will-formation, is ongoing. So we may ask: Is not the fostering of the *capacity* for doubt a key—although not exclusive—part of the civic value of a core text education?

Works Cited

Alighieri, Dante. *The Divine Comedy*. Trans. Mark Musa. New York: Penguin, 1984. Print.

Arendt, Hannah. *The Human Condition*. Chicago: U of Chicago P, 1958. Print.

Tocqueville and the Problem of Associational Autonomy

Thomas (Tom) M.J. Bateman
St. Thomas University

Contemporary liberal democracies grapple with a dilemma going to their core commitments. They protect a catalogue of freedoms including freedom of association. This is an individual right but with implications for the ability of individuals to unite for purposes of their choosing and according to principles of organization and governance that seem best to them. Freedom of association is the legal foundation for the flourishing of civil society for which liberal democracies are so well known.

What is at stake, however, if civil associations themselves depart from the principles of liberal democracy? For example, a church may operate according to principles that fail to recognize full sexual equality for purposes of the ministry. It may refuse to ordain female pastors or priests. A sexual assault counseling centre may have a policy according to which only women may be hired as counselors. A private golf club may refuse membership to women. A private university may require students and faculty to sign a statement committing them to abstain from premarital and homosexual sexual activity. A church may refuse to rent its facilities for the celebration of same-sex marriages. A sports association may only allow girls to play hockey in its league. That same association may forbid girls from wearing hijabs or chadors while playing sports.

How shall a liberal democracy respond to these circumstances? One response is to do nothing unless associations exert coercive power over their members. Albert Hirschman's famous three-fold set of options should, on this view, always be open to members of associations: exit, voice, and loyalty (Hirschman). If an association becomes intolerable for a member, that member should always be able to speak up and/or leave. Thus associations are given a wide berth and *in extremis* are limited by the liberal democratic principle of individual freedom, the ability to dissociate being an aspect of the ability to associate. In other words, as long as civil associations stop short of exercising coercive state powers themselves, they can operate in a liberal democracy. Associational freedom here means a robust, deep associational diversity (Gray). Liberal democracy is a dense, unkempt wood—a riot of color and leaf, some weeds and brambles, but also majestic trees and extraordinary ferns.

A very different response is to act on a concern that liberal democracies are like fragile gardens that need constant attention. All flowers in the garden must be tended. There can be no weeds. All the flowers must contribute to the ordered beauty of the whole. Left unattended, weeds in the corner will grow uncontrollably and crowd out the beautiful flowers. The garden will in time be ugly, unruly, and dangerous. No one will want to visit it. Like the flowers in the garden, associations must be monitored and steered. Most importantly, the liberal democratic values that govern the regime must penetrate "all the way down" into the associational life of civil society. Citizens in their private lives should embody and live out the principles of equality, non-discrimination, fairness, and due process that obtain in public life (Macedo). Private life will mirror public life because public values will be private values. Like charity, liberal democratic principles, as it were, begin at home. But we have to make sure that homes are structured so that the liberal democratic virtues do indeed begin there. Liberal democratic regimes must have liberal democratic associations that produce liberal democratic individuals.

But what of freedom? This second response to associational illiberalism sounds like it is interested in destroying the regime in order to save it. Are associations prisons from which people need to be liberated? If so, who does the liberating? Or are associations the very stuff of freedom, to be protected from the good intentions of the liberators? These are hard questions, and contemporary politicians are usually afraid to address them. They become legal issues. But the courts are also having difficulties. Fortunately thoughtful observers have considered these questions. Alexis de Tocqueville is one of them. His magisterial *Democracy in America* is worth examining.

***

Tocqueville's study is as much of democracy as it is of democracy in America. While, as he says, America's particular institutional forms and laws are not to be imitated by others, many of his observations are transferable. His chief observation is that while democracy's virtues are obvious and trumpeted by many, its perils are little known and even less remarked. Democracy is guided by the hand of Providence, and there is no turning back to aristocracy. But democracy needs statesmanlike stewardship to prevent it from descending into despotism. Americans love liberty. They also love equality. Forced to choose between the two, they will take equality, not least because equality gives each a share in the formation of the laws and in the formation of the opinion of the majority. Equality seems, then, to foreclose tyranny or oligarchy. In this sense, equality is more important than liberty but at the same time seems to safeguard liberty.

Alas, it is not so simple. Americans desire well being and love material enjoyments. These become their principal preoccupations and fuel the practical enterprises of American commerce. The pursuit of such enjoyments leads them away from public affairs and the needs of their fellows. They become individualistic; each is disposed to "isolate himself from the mass of those like him and to withdraw to one side with his family and his friends, so that after having thus created a little society for his own use, he willingly abandons society at large to itself" (II.2.2, 482). Each defers to the majority, that imperious intellectual and moral authority. It becomes a tyranny of the majority, but the individualistic citizen is unconcerned: he is weak, isolated, shapeless, while it is strong. The majority rules not by restraint but by gentle persuasion. The law goes to the body; the opinion of the majority goes straight to the soul (II.3.21).

Democracy enters a "perilous passage": if love of well being is too intense and unaccompanied by enlightenment, people will give up civil and political freedom to get it. They forget that their principal affair is "to remain masters of themselves" and will give themselves over to those who would assist them in their headlong desire for comfort and enjoyment (II.2.14, 515). Americans then lower their standards for political life. They become content merely with public order and tranquility. But most regimes can deliver this. Indeed, democracy is often agitated and unstable, given to new laws and innovations. Gentle public administration seems preferable. They deliver themselves to a gentle, mild government that promises to take care of them. They demand more of it and less of themselves and others. In the end, the farmer will want the head of government to come down and himself take the plow (II.2.5, 491). The people become a "herd of timid and industrious animals of which the government is the shepherd" (II.4.6, 663).

Associational life is caught up in this process of decline. In several places Tocqueville describes the inter-penetration of the public and private realms. Some of the habits of private life are carried into public life; commercial forms in private seep into public priorities (1.2.5). The obverse is also evident, and Tocqueville seems to think that democratic ideas more powerfully flow down from the public realm than associational ideas flow up from the private realm. "[T]he republic," he writes, "penetrates, if I can express myself so, the ideas, opinions, and all the habits of the Americans at the same time as it establishes itself in their laws; and to come to change the laws, [the Americans] would have to come in a way to the point of wholly changing themselves. In the United States, even the religion of the greatest number is itself republican" (1.2.10, 381). Democratic mores have penetrated "little by little into usages, into opinions, into forms: it is found in all the details of social life as in the laws" (1.2.9, 294–5).

It appears that the inter-penetration of public and private is as natural to democracy as is democracy's own descent into despotism. Indeed, the former conduces to and is a part of the latter movement downward.

***

Only by political art can both descents be avoided. Among the arts of liberty such as the judicial enforcement of the rule of law, a free press, religion and especially the Christian religion, and local government (the "secondary powers" between central government and the citizen), association is nearly the most important. "Among the laws that rule human societies there is one that seems more precise and clearer than all the others. In order that men remain civilized or become so," Tocqueville urges, "the art of associating must be developed and perfected among them in the same ratio as equality of conditions increases" (II.2.5, 492). Association draws the individualist outside of himself, showing him the needs of others and teaching him the arts of public action. Associations multiply the strength of weak individuals. They give people the means to resist overweening government. They are the stuff of freedom.

Tocqueville's language suggests that the democratic statesman must follow a policy on associational vitality. He does indicate that the art of association must be "developed." What does such a policy look like? Does it require an active intervention into associational life to stimulate associational activity, to reduce in number and severity its unpalatable manifestations, to direct associational activities to ends the statesman thinks worthy? Should the state fund certain associational activities to reduce barriers to entry?

If the statesman follows these courses, do associations remain associations in the Tocquevillian sense? How much encouragement or guidance can proceed from the state before it transforms associations into organs of the state?

Tocqueville's comments on religion in America are perhaps instructive. Religion, particularly Christianity, is important, according to Tocqueville, because it gives people an abiding sense of the transcendent and immaterial to balance their obsessions with material enjoyments. American Christianity supports democracy by fostering a stable, egalitarian morality in which family life is honored and women exalted. American religion is disestablished and thus it appears in an associational form. In its dominant Protestant guise, Christianity's institutional character mirrors that of the township: local governance, lay participation, and vigorous defense of independence, both individual and corporate. "Despotism can do without faith," he writes, "but freedom cannot" (I.2.9, 282). But here is the key: Christianity is vital and powerful in American life precisely because it lacks political power. It is the separation of church and state that redounds to the advantage of the church (I.2.9). Given the separation of church and state, the statesman can do precious little to foster religious faith and practice. Tocqueville's prescription: "I believe that the only efficacious means governments can use to put the dogma of the immortality of the soul in honor is to act every day as if they themselves believed it; and I think it is only in conforming themselves scrupulously to religious morality in great affairs that they can flatter themselves they are teaching citizens to know it, love it, and respect it at all times" (II.2.15, 521). In like manner, perhaps Tocqueville recommends that statesmen appear to foster state support for associational life, when in fact they must preserve the autonomy of associations for the very health and vitality of those associations.

***

If all associations are like religious associations in fundamental respects, the policy of the statesman is perhaps the scrupulous avoidance of state interference in associational life. Democracies will need to prefer the unkempt wood to the domesticated order of the garden. The paradox in all this is that for the regime as a whole, it is harder to leave associational life to its own devices than it is to prune and cultivate it. We always want government to *do something*. And politicians have short term incentives to grant our wish. But then, as Tocqueville remarked, "There is nothing more prolific in marvels than the art of being free; but there is nothing harder than the apprenticeship of freedom" (1.2.6, 229).

Contemporary observers may not be convinced of Tocqueville's *laissez-faire* approach to associational life. They believe government is a helper, not a dominator. They also believe America is a more complex, diverse society than the unified one of Tocqueville's day. Tocqueville does not solve the problem for us, but he does suggest what is at stake when we propose solutions. Students of democracy, social capital, and civil and human rights would all do well to return to *Democracy in America*.

Works Cited

Gray, John. 2000. *Two Faces of Liberalism*. New York: The New Press, 2000.

Hirschman, Albert O. *Exit, Voice, and Loyalty: Response to Declines in Firms, Organizations, and States*. Cambridge, MA: Harvard UP, 1970.

Macedo, Stephen. *Diversity and Distrust: Civic Education in Multicultural Democracy*. Cambridge, MA: Harvard UP, 2000.

Tocqueville, Alexis de. *Democracy in America*. Trans. Harvey C. Mansfield and Delba Winthrop. Chicago: Chicago UP, 2000.

Teaching About Evil and Politics Using Elie Wiesel's *Night*

Tim Meinke
Lynchburg College

In his Nobel Peace Prize acceptance speech, President Obama stated firmly: "make no mistake: evil does exist in the world." And no matter what they came to think of his "axis of evil" policies, very few Americans disagreed with President Bush on the night of 9/11 when he told us: "Today, our nation saw evil." In each of these speeches, first-term Presidents of different parties were comfortable enough with the concept of evil to use the term several times. Obviously, each believed it would convey a powerful message to his global audience. This suggests that humans accept both the existence of evil and its impact on our politics, yet we rarely think about, much less study, evil as a political or social phenomenon. On flipping through any college catalogue one would not be surprised to find Philosophy, Religious Studies, or Literature classes on evil, but it would be surprising to find social science offerings on the topic. If we accept the existence of such a phenomenon, and leave the debate over the root of evil to the theologians, then political scientists are left to answer: what is the impact of evil on the collective actions of humans in the political realm?

This paper will begin with a brief description of one course taught at Lynchburg College that aims to engage students in answering this question, but will focus on the use of the core text *Night* by Elie Wiesel to advance this goal. The course employs the social science method of indirect observation to answer the question by assigning students a number of readings, such as *Night*, that relate, in their own words, the experiences of either victims or killers during situations that most everyone would label as evil. Genocide is one of those political situations that most everyone feels comfortable describing as evil, so the course uses two case studies of genocide in the twentieth century, the attempted destruction of European Jewry in Poland during the 1940s and the mass murder of Tutsis in Rwanda during 1994, as the basis for the semester's work. Using readings from both victims and killers, students are encouraged through a variety of assignments to look for patterns that help to answer the following questions: How do we know when we are dealing with evil in our midst? What is the impact of evil on our political interactions? And what are the best ways to deal with evil in our midst?

The course is divided into six sections. After a one-class introduction to the concept of genocide, students are introduced to the overall methodology of the course by reading *Night* and spending a couple class sessions discussing the characteristics of the situation lived by Wiesel. The second section offers students a few brief encounters with varying perspectives on evil by spending two weeks on readings from the Bible, literature, and the social sciences. Students read the story of the creation and fall of humans in Genesis and the whole book of Job, and discuss the Christian understanding of evil. Next students read and discuss an interesting short story, "The White People," written in 1899 by Arthur Machen. In the story, Ambrose argues that evil is misunderstood socially because people equate it with bad things such as murder when true evil is an attempt to penetrate a higher sphere that is off limits for humans. The section ends with selections from two of the few social science works addressing evil: Fred Alford's *What Evil Means to Us* and M. Scott Peck's *People of the Lie: The Hope for Healing Human Evil*. Using very different methodologies, each concluded that evil actions are attempts by an individual to escape their own humanity. Peck argued evil-doers could be described as malignant narcissists who attack others rather than deal with their own failures. Alford found that evil actions come from our sense of dread over the possibility of not-being and our lack of control in the matter; he argued evil-doers were attempting to control this dread by inflicting it on others. However, with the exception of Peck's chapter 6 on My Lai and group evil, both works deal with evil from the individual perspective rather than explore it from a group or political perspective.

The third section gets students to think about the need for government power to control these evil impulses in individual human beings. They read Cormac McCarthy's Pulitzer Prize winning novel *The Road* and the section on the state of nature from Thomas Hobbes' *Leviathan* to gain an appreciation of life without government. At the end of the section they read chapters 17 and 18 from *Leviathan* on Hobbes' solution for such a state of nature, which is an extremely powerful government with the ability to keep all individuals in such awe that they will behave.

The next two sections of the course focus on the two case studies of genocide in the twentieth century and demonstrate the possible problem with Hobbes's solution: what happens when the government power, made up of human beings capable of evil, becomes evil or acts in an evil manner? The answer is that 6 million Jews can be killed in a few years or 800,000 to a million Tutsis can be eliminated in 100 days. To explore these two cases from the perspectives of both the victims and killers, students read both primary and secondary sources. For the case study of the Holocaust, students read Hannah Arendt's *Eichmann and the Holocaust*, which is a shortened version of her classic *Eichmann in Jerusalem: A Report on the Banality of Evil*. They also read and discuss Primo Levi's concept of "The Grey Zone" from *The Drowned and the Saved* and Christopher Browning's *Ordinary Men*. For the Rwanda case study, the students read two excellent works by the French journalist Jean Hatzfeld, who has spent considerable time in Rwanda interviewing both victims and killers. In one book, *Machete Season: The Killers in Rwanda Speak*, students are introduced to ten killers from the Nyamata district and in the other, *Life Laid Bare: The Survivors in Rwanda Speak*, they learn the stories of fourteen survivors from all over the country in their own words. In the final section of the class, students are encouraged to think about lessons for surviving evil in our midst by reading Viktor Frankl's Man's *Search for Meaning* and Immaculée Ilibagiza's *Left to Tell*.

The course opens with *Night* because Wiesel's writing is easy to understand and the book is short, yet his experiences are shared with such vividness that it is as if the reader is observing as "[a] young Jewish boy discovered the Kingdom of Night" (Wiesel, 118). Most importantly, his experiences offer answers to the central questions of the class that can subsequently be seen in the other accounts read later in the semester. For example, we learn from reading Wiesel's account that life in the midst of evil is marked by total loneliness or complete alienation from other human beings. A strong sense of separation between oppressor and oppressed is not surprising, but it is surprising to note that in the midst of evil individuals feel a profound sense of separation from everything and everyone on the world. Wiesel's description of his emotional state on Rosh Hashanah 1944 is a good illustration: "My eyes had opened and I was alone, terribly alone in a world without God, without man. Without love or mercy" (Wiesel, 68). Most importantly, this alienation even includes our most beloved friends and family. Obviously, the bond between Elie and his father was immensely strong and based on deep respect and affection, but there were many times when young Elie felt as he did after their first shower in Auschwitz: "I wanted to tell him [father] something, but I didn't know what" (Wiesel, 37). It was as if the bonds of communication were even broken between father and son.

Second, in the midst of evil, victims of terrible crimes are stripped of their innocence as they enter what Primo Levi in *The Drowned and the Saved* (1989) described as the "gray zone." If a terrible event happens, such as losing one's home during a bombing raid, that person is treated with pity and feels no guilt, but in evil situations we find that even the oppressed lose such a sense of victimhood. In *Night*, Wiesel often discusses the guilt he felt over what he did or did not do in the concentration camp. As he relates their first night in a barracks he tells the story of his father being beaten for asking where the toilets were and remembers that: "My father had just been struck, in front of me, and I had not even blinked" (Wiesel, 39). As Levi tell us, this does not mean that Elie should be held responsible for what happened to his father, but it does prevent him from feeling, acting, and being treated like the victim he was. This "grey zone" is most dramatically illustrated in the story of Bela Katz, who had arrived at Auschwitz one week before the Wiesels and who was selected as one of the *Sonderkommandos*, whose task it was to transport bodies from the gas chambers to the crematoria. At one point he slipped a note to the Wiesels and told them, "that having been chosen because of his strength, he had been forced to place his own father's body into the furnace" (Wiesel, 35). Again, young Katz was not his father's murderer, but we can only imagine the torment in which he lived out his last days.

Another characteristic of evil discovered in *Night* is that banal actions by ordinary humans lead to spectacular, unnatural results. This is illustrated by the horrible recounting of Elie's last moment with his mother and sister: "Men to the left. Women to the right. Eight simple, short words. Yet that was the moment when I left my mother" (Wiesel, 29). A few moments later, Elie and his father witness another illustration as guards driving trucks, a very ordinary action, are bringing babies to be burned in open fire pits. It was too much for a young boy to process and led to him crying out to his father that he "could not believe that human beings were being burned in our times; the world would never tolerate such crimes" (Wiesel, 33). Elie's father's reaction to the sight of babies being burned illustrates yet another characteristic of living in the midst of evil. As he responds to his young son by exclaiming, "The world? The world is not interested in us. Today, everything is possible, even the crematoria" (Wiesel, 33), he is explaining that evil actions are marked by an irrational lack of limits.

Finally, Wiesel's account of his experiences also suggests that while political might is necessary to fight evil, the ultimate solution may lie with individuals who are thoughtful, loving, and able to persevere in the belief that goodness is worth fighting for. We find support for this in the relationship between Elie and his father, which is clearly the only reason that either makes it to 1945 and that Elie survives the war. For example, as Elie is contemplating suicide on the Death March of January 1945, he finds that "My father's presence was the only thing that stopped me" (Wiesel, 86). Also, neither would have survived the first selection at Auschwitz if not for the kindness of a stranger who told them that it would be wise to lie about their ages. This suggests that if we are really serious about dealing with political evil in our midst we must challenge each other to never forget these events, so that we remember human beings are capable of both profound good and evil. We must learn to recognize the characteristics of evil in our midst and realize that our own thoughtfulness and love for others might be the best defense against such evil.

Works Cited

Levi, Primo. *The Drowned and the Saved.* Trans. Raymond Rosenthal. New York: Vintage, 1989.

Wiesel, Elie. *Night.* Trans. Marion Wiesel. New York: Hill and Wang, 2006.

Part VI. Moral Images of Humankind

Using Nussbaum to Link Socrates, *Tartuffe*, and *Raise the Red Lantern* with Today's Global Citizen

Kathleen A. Kelly
Babson College

In foundation courses where one of the goals is to educate for global citizenship, Plato's *Apology* and *Crito* can be powerful texts. Socrates makes of his own death a testimony to the obligation citizens have to think critically and act courageously against injustices. At the same time, his reverence for the laws of the city, even when a majority opinion has just unfairly sentenced him to death, can be a good starting point for exploring what love of country, or patriotism, actually entails. Despite Socrates' powerful example, however, these valuable lessons may be too easily relegated to the remote past. How might today's student appropriate critical thinking and the "examined life" as Socrates models them? A brief article by Martha Nussbaum, "Education for Profit, Education for Freedom," can amplify the significance of Socrates' challenge to students by making its relevance to their own context more apparent and by putting it more readily into conversation with other core texts from very different contexts. I will illustrate with reference to Molière's *Tartuffe* and Zhang Yimou's film *Raise the Red Lantern.*

Socrates assumes a relatively small, direct democracy in which every citizen is expected to be a lawmaker and hold public office; everyone must think critically, then, for the fate of his city depends on it. But in the large nation states most of our students inhabit, citizens are not directly involved in lawmaking and are rarely involved in judicial decisions. The examined life that is so important to Socrates in his self-appointed role as gadfly to the state, then, may not seem so relevant to students' own contexts. And even if the reader entertains the challenge to lead the examined life, how much of a challenge is it? After all, in these two dialogues, Socrates' focus for the examined life seems primarily on examining other people's lives, other people's faulty thinking and emotional decision making. Who, listening to Socrates' account, actually sees himself in the position of the politician, the poet, and the artisan who claim to know more than they actually do? Even Crito's more well-meaning logical fallacies are not so difficult for the reader to expose. Certainly we are impressed by Socrates' ability to make fools of his malicious accusers, to lead such a one down the garden path and into a logical trap. His own self-examining, however, seems to have happened already, calmly beforehand, so that he might come across as almost inhumanly rationale, as Crito remarks. In other words, Socrates' life and death as represented in these two dialogues are compelling testimony to the importance *he* places on living the examined life, but does it persuade us that our own lives are unexamined, that we need to think all that much harder to understand what justice entails? In a first-year course, without the leisure to conduct a full-scale analysis of several Platonic dialogues that would elaborate Socrates' challenge, Martha Nussbaum's essay not only can provide a compelling argument for the value of the liberal education in general, but can also help students specifically to appreciate the relevance of Socrates' challenge.

Just as Socrates proposes that an educator understand "the proper qualities for human beings and for citizens" (*Apology*, 20b) so Nussbaum proposes that we assume education must promote the human development of students as global citizens. An education that puts human development first, freedom rather than profit, will have as its goal "producing decent world citizens who can understand . . . global problems" in the light of justice, "and who have the practical competence and the motivational incentives to do something about those problems." Nussbaum elaborates three requirements for such an education—Socratic self-criticism, an understanding of diversity, and "narrative imagination." For my purposes, however, even more helpful than her discussion of what an education for human development entails is her explanation for why we need to be *educated* for justice and equality at all. Isn't it obvious that we should all be fair and reasonable? Don't we all, at least usually, feel that we behave that way? Only malicious libelers such as Meletus, or friends overcome by grief such as Crito, behave badly. Nussbaum, however, describes several factors, structural and psychological, that make it difficult for everyone, no matter how enlightened, to sustain egalitarian institutions.

Outlining the structural barriers to equality, Nussbaum notes that we all have a tendency to defer to authority and to be susceptible to peer pressure; when cast in a dominant role we can readily be taught to believe in the inferiority of others; and we are more likely to behave badly when we are put into a role where we are not held accountable. Psychologically, human beings want to transcend their mortality and finitude and to be omnipotent, yet in reality we are often powerlessness, and this can result in anxiety, shame, and revulsion at our own imperfection. As history records, shame and revulsion "are all too often projected outward onto subordinate groups who can conveniently symbolize [these] problematic aspects." We also have a tendency to want to see others not as equal subjects but merely as a means to our own satisfaction. To treat others as subjects in their own right, global citizens must learn to see others' subjectivities as equal to their own. An education for freedom, then, must engender knowledge about those subjectivities and cultivate the imagination to be able to empathize with them.

Nussbaum's *explicit* attention to the human tendencies that inhibit critical thinking for justice complement Socrates' assessment of his fellow citizens' uncritical thinking and bad behavior—the envy, hatred, slander, or passion that Socrates exposes. She helps students see that challenges to critical thinking might readily come from within themselves as well as existing in others. Focusing on the barriers to thinking critically also makes it easier to build a bridge from Socrates' concerns for justice to an examination of justice in other texts that emerge from contexts radically different from Athens' direct democracy. This range can be suggested by a look at Molière's *Tartuffe* written in the context of Louis XIV's absolute monarchy, and Zhang Yimou's *Raise the Red Lantern,* a 1991 film released in the wake of the Tiananmen Square massacre. A primary focus for both of these narratives is the structural and psychological barriers that lead well-meaning people to act unjustly, whether they are in a position of power or of subservience.

In *Tartuffe,* Orgon is the epitome of the character who believes himself to be reasonable, just, and good, especially in relation to his own family. We readily see, however, that his unrecognized fears and his authoritative position blind him to how outrageously unfair he actually is. He is so concerned about the salvation of his family members, he tells himself, that he takes in the preacher Tartuffe to watch over them. In particular, he is interested in having Tartuffe keep an eye on his young wife's social life, and in marrying Tartuffe to his daughter, thereby preventing her, as well as his son, from leaving his household. It is obvious to most everyone in the family, and certainly to the audience, that Orgon is being duped by Tartuffe, who lusts after Orgon's wife and his estate. Much comic laughter derives from Orgon's refusal to believe what is directly before him, and the scene in which Orgon only reluctantly emerges from under the table to save his wife from Tartuffe's lecherous advances on top, is justly renowned.

Why does Orgon persist in his blindness? Although Orgon is far removed both from Socrates' direct democracy and from today's global citizen, we can nevertheless readily analyze his behavior in Socrates' and Nussbaum's terms. Structurally, within the patriarchy ruled over by the absolute monarch Louis XIV, Orgon is king in his own household, and although he is expected to abide by reasonable social norms, no one within has the authority to hold him accountable. The irrepressible maid, Dorine, is perhaps the most reasonable character in the play, but she has the least authority, and Orgon goes to great, and comical, trouble to keep her quiet. Why doesn't Orgon act the benevolent patriarch that he believes himself to be? Psychologically, as the aging paterfamilias with a young wife and children on the verge of leaving his household to marry, Orgon feels himself losing control over his family. This fear of powerlessness makes him an easy target for the unscrupulous Tartuffe, who implicitly promises Orgon God's authority in exerting his will. In the end, Orgon is saved from his unreason only by the figure of the all-knowing monarch, whose deputy arrests Tartuffe and restores Orgon's property. This homage to his monarch insures Molière against any charge of sedition, but by representing the profound susceptibility of a patriarch to the structural and psychological barriers that cause injustice, the play speaks both to its own times and to our own, particularly to the importance of critical self-awareness, empathy, and knowledge of the histories of human injustice and fallibility.

Situated in a very different time and place, Zhang Yimou's *Raise the Red Lantern* also represents a patriarchal system, but here the film focuses not on the fallible Master of the household but on the subordinate women who miss opportunities to cultivate justice within the strictures of the system. The entire film unfolds in the enclosed (architecturally exquisite) compound of its wealthy Master, where patriarchal tradition and custom reign supreme. The young protagonist, Songlian, has agreed to rescue her family from destitution by becoming the fourth wife, "Fourth Mistress" as the English subtitles term it, of this Master. With her, we gradually discover that the customs in this compound function to keep the mistresses in perpetual rivalry for the favors of the Master.

Specifically, the Master's selection of which mistress he will bed with that night is heralded every evening by a parade of bright red lanterns into the favored mistress's courtyard. As long as she remains the favored mistress, she enjoys exceptional deference in all areas of compound life—deference required from the three other mistresses as well as from the servants. Before arriving, Songlian exhibited a strong, independent spirit, but once she learns that all favors descend from the favor of the Master, she quickly succumbs to the system. In order to remain in the Master's favor, she uses her feisty spirit not against the Master and his customs, but against the other mistresses and her own maid. Only after Songlian's harsh treatment leads to her maid's death, and her drunken talk leads to the Master's execution of Third Mistress, does Songlian seem to recognize her essential equality with these women. After secretly witnessing the execution of Third Mistress, she refuses to keep quiet, screaming "Murderers, Murderers," and goes on to frighten everyone in the compound by "haunting" Third Mistress's quarters. These protests are short-lived, however, and Songlian falls into despair and madness. Her essential powerlessness at the end is highlighted by the arrival of Fifth Mistress, with all the welcoming ceremonies with which she herself had been received only a year earlier.

Young Songlian is clearly a victim of an oppressive system, but the film focuses much more on the destructive responses that the women, and Songlian in particular, have to that situation and on the opportunities lost. Instead of seeing that the rivalries among the mistresses have been created by a history that is repeating itself through her, Songlian considers herself better and above the first three mistresses, and she flaunts the power that the Master's initial favor gives her. Instead of using her "narrative imagination" to see that her maid is in a situation very similar to her own, Songlian taunts and abuses her. She is unable to imagine that there might be opportunities to work with these women against the Master by defusing rivalries and using what little agency they have to try to support each other.

Although set in 1920s China, the film invites metaphorical rather than historical readings. It can be seen as a veiled reference to the relation Chinese citizens have to "an authoritarian government that allows no freedom of expression"—the film was banned in China when it was released in 1991 (Neo). It can also, however, reference any tyranny, even the "soft tyranny" of the Western bureaucratic state and the free market, insofar as these might lead us to believe that the systems we live in are beyond our control or that our only effective self-expression is through consumption and creating envy in others.

The story of Socrates' trial and death makes a compelling case for the importance of living a just life and actively opposing injustice. Martha Nussbaum's explanation for why we must be educated to overcome the structural and psychological barriers to sustaining justice strongly amplifies Socrates' message, linking it directly to the concerns of other core texts and of the global citizens in our classrooms.

Works Cited

Molière. *The Misanthrope and Tartuffe*. Trans. Richard Wilbur. New York: Harcourt, 1965.

Neo, David. "The 'Confucian Ethics' of *Raise the Red Lantern*." *Senses of Cinema* *51* (2004): n.p.

Nussbaum, Martha. "Education for Profit, Education for Freedom." *Liberal Education* 95. 3 (2009): n.p.

Plato's Euthyphro, Apology, Crito, Phaedo. Trans. Benjamin Jowett, rev. trans. Albert A. Anderson. Millis: Agora, 2005.

Raise the Red Lantern. Dir. Zhang Yimou. Perf. Gong Li, Ma Jingwu. 1991. MGM, 2007. DVD.

Novel Knowledge in Turgenev's *Fathers and Sons*

James N. Roney
Juniata College

Why read novels in a core course? One common answer is novels are an effective means to important ends: either the content or reality depicted in the novel or the critical thinking and other skills one acquires by reading and writing about it. In either case, the novel is valuable not in itself but for the interaction it facilitates with something more important. If another simpler or more entertaining means to the same content or skill could be found, then there would be no reason to read the novel. Anyone who has taken part in curricular discussions knows that this argument often results in complex core texts losing their place in a course. However, if novels contain knowledge or experience specific to them and if the aesthetic perception and intellectual attention required to understand them is unique, then they are not means but ends in themselves. They contribute either an experiential awareness of the meaningfulness of life (Eldridge, Ingarden) or insight into the uncertain ambiguity of individual existence (Kundera) while allowing us to develop the moral empathy necessary to understand life from others' perspectives and act responsibly in the world as moral agents whose fuller awareness of how others will perceive and react to our actions increases our sense of pragmatic consequences (Bakhtin, *Problems;* Nussbaum). Novels should remain in core courses because the aesthetic perception they provide makes us better, more effective people.

Ivan Turgenev's novel *Fathers and Sons* is widely used in Russian history courses to introduce students to the key debates of Russian nineteenth-century intellectual life. When used in a core course, it also poses fundamental questions about the proper balance between commitment to reform based on the truth as one sees it and respect for others' beliefs, about the value of science and its relationship to other forms of knowledge, and about happiness and life itself. The aesthetic way in which Turgenev answers these questions demonstrates the value of novels as means for the emotional and intellectual apprehension of human experience.

Turgenev wrote his novel in 1862, setting it a few years earlier on the eve of the abolition of serfdom. He analyzed a new social type, a revolutionary representative of the newly educated lower classes who was a student of the natural sciences and dismissive of all the learning and social conventions Turgenev's older liberal generation had respected (Berlin). Turgenev coined the term "nihilist" to describe this new movement:

> "What is Bazarov?" Arkady smiled. "Would you like me to tell you, uncle, what he is exactly?"
>
> "Please do, nephew."
>
> "He is a nihilist!"
>
> "A what?" asked Nikolai Petrovich, while his brother lifted his knife in the air with a small piece of butter on the tip and remained motionless.
>
> "He is a nihilist," repeated Arkady.
>
> "A nihilist," said Nikolai Petrovich. "That comes from the Latin *nihil-nothing*. I imagine: the term must signify a man who…who recognizes nothing?"
>
> "Say—who respects nothing," put in Pavel Petrovich, and set to work with the butter again.
>
> "Who looks at everything critically," observed Arkady. (Turgenev 94)

The novel presents intellectual debate and social conflict as lived human experience. The butter hangs in the air, suspended on the knife, as all wait for a response. The uncle can butter his roll only after he has classified the new phenomenon. The father's pain at losing contact with his son is real: the aristocratic son is both proud and vaguely uneasy about enjoying his superiority over his father; underlying class hostility might be motivating the debate over ideas between the most aggressive representatives of the older and younger generations. This human context and the aesthetic experience it evokes become more important than the philosophical dispute, culminating in the famously enigmatic final lines: "However passionate, sinful, and rebellious the heart hidden in the tomb, the flowers growing over it peep at us serenely with their innocent eyes: they speak to us not only of eternal peace, of the vast repose of 'indifferent' nature: they tell us, too, of everlasting reconciliation and of life which has no end" (Turgenev 294).

Turgenev absorbs his famous nihilist and scientific revolutionary, Bazarov, into the world of the novel even as the earth absorbs Bazarov into the flow of nature. The novel both protests a world that overcomes the most energetic character, thwarting a necessary social change, and asserts that life, nature, and art contain a life principle the young nihilist never understood. Turgenev's contemporaries saw his novel as an act in the cultural conflict over the materialist philosophy and revolutionary activism of the 1860s. The generation of the 1840s lived through the Russian version of the European debate between enlightened liberalism and romantic nationalism. Turgenev's "fathers" (often called Westernizers) believed in the importance of enlightened civilization to a society in which the rights of the privileged would be gradually extended to all. They valued philosophy, music, and art. Their opponents, the Slavophiles, believed the communal life of the Russian peasantry had preserved the Russian soul and unique traditions of Russian Orthodoxy while valuing the artistic and philosophical traditions of European romanticism. The "sons" (Turgenev's nihilists) rejected this entire debate, turning instead to scientific materialism and rational egotism. Seeing life as a struggle of wills in which only results matter and only the strong survive, they rejected all art and philosophy as meaningless and called for an immediate, total transformation of Russian society.

Early in the novel Turgenev represents the social changes surrounding the emancipation of the serfs and the battle over materialism as a generational conflict. The fathers, the brothers Nikolai and Pavel Kirsanov, believe in liberal principles, art, and philosophy. Nikolai has changed his estate from one based on the number of laboring serfs into a farm, measured in acres, whose peasants pay rent and receive their own land. Pavel manicures his nails and retains all the aristocratic dress of the English nobles whose respect for their own rights and responsibilities he views as the only basis for democratic respect for the rights of others. The younger generation, Arkady, and Bazarov, reject all art and all principles and argue for total commitment to reform in a world composed only of warring egos and ideas. They replace Nikolai's poetry book with a popular chemistry text. They claim to be beyond the mystical aura of romantic love, seeing it as only a natural function. Pavel and Bazarov duel both verbally and physically as their differences become irreconcilable. Nikolai senses the slaveholder in himself and concludes that the time of his generation has passed. Pavel's reaction to the young radicals is strong enough that he switches sides in the debate of the 40s: the nihilist threat to the enlightened liberalism he once espoused is so severe that he becomes a Slavophile, arguing the peasants will preserve Russia by rejecting Bazarov. The generational split is different for the Odintsova sisters: Anna has the older generation's respect for social form, but Katya is certainly no nihilist.

The architectural settings and cultural space of the novel also mirror the philosophical debate as surface changes mask deeper continuities. The Odintsova estate runs with the perfect order of the older classical aristocracy's unchanging system. Bazarov's mother is an ancient Russian woman, hearkening back to even older forms. The liberal reforms have shaken the order of the Kirsanov estate, but the rhythms of noble life in the countryside continue and are even strengthened by the new married couples at the end. The scenes in the city provide satires on emancipated women, liberal officials who are autocrats with new vocabulary, and sons of alcohol merchants who seek a new status by claiming allegiance to the latest ideas.

Turgenev prevents an allegorical reading of the novel by contrasting this social debate with the human experience unfolding within it. Arkady initially views his home region with disgust as a place that has only recently escaped from the grip of a beast that could be either winter or serfdom. He says it must all change at once. However, signs of spring immediately enter his consciousness, and he becomes joyfully aware of nature's new life, causing his father to embrace him and start reciting poetry (Turgenev 83). Readers have to ask: Are both of these two realities real? Should we dedicate ourselves to the joy of being alive in the company of individuals we know or to the cause of transforming an alienated present? Arkady might not understand himself and may be more like his father than like his young nihilist mentor. Turgenev uses all of his talent to describe Nature, which the nihilists held to be a workshop and not a temple, in aesthetically powerful terms. Roman Ingarden argued art allows us to experience life as meaningful by providing perceptions of really existing meaningful states or metaphysical essences (Ingarden). Turgenev fills his novel with such meaningful natural scenes, regrouping his characters into those who are and are not capable of experiencing them.

Pavel, Anna, and Bazarov are incapable of experiencing not only the beauty of nature but also love, music, and poetry. In one famous scene, Anna coerces and then fearfully rejects Bazarov's declaration of love. The open window, her fully clothed body, and her fear of drafts show her fear of unknown vitality and need for the ordered shell of a routine. Nikolai, Arkady, and Katya, on the other hand, appreciate art, nature and love, even when Arkady's ideology makes him deny his own experience. Characters who are open to the things valued by the earlier romanticism are the only ones who are happy in life. The metaphysical essence of being for them is one of vital plenitude leading to joy, children, and marriage. The other characters sense a void at the center of existence, filling it with rules, ideas, and principles over which they will fight because without them there is only "Mongolian chaos" (Turgenev 127). Pavel does this with his English habits; Anna uses the clockwork mechanism of her orderly estate to make time pass without notice; Bazarov's nihilism may ironically be his search for a single principle to order the chaotic struggle for existence and oppose the Russian social system that excludes him from a meaningful life. Is there a fatalistic individualism here? Are some people born to happiness? Are others born to an alienated life held together by social form? Does each person have a basic character that is more important than philosophical beliefs or generational membership in determining the course of our life? Are some born to be the heroes of their own comedies, enjoying the organic fullness of family life, while others play in tragedies, confronting an existential void with abstract ideas, commitments to social causes, and orderly rituals? Given the vagaries of human character, do we need to rethink the universal assumptions about human nature at the core of the debate over nihilism?

Characters come to important individual realizations. Bazarov confronts the horror of his own insignificance and failed ambition to change the world and dies with true heroism, attempting to console his father and be completely honest with the woman he loved who never loved him. Odintsova apparently accepts her own inability to love and marries a liberal lawyer out of a sense of duty. Katya and Arkady accept who they are and live a rural family life. Pavel tells Nikolai to marry the beloved peasant mother of his child before accepting his own status as an elegant émigré. Nikolai himself becomes a happy, rural paterfamilias. All of these decisions share a recognition of the human dimension of life, an awareness that an individual life as lived is more complicated than university lectures and abstract principles, and the problematic knowledge that some mysterious force demands reconciliation even as it unfairly splits us into the spontaneously happy and the stoically accepting of the void at the center of some individual lives.

In summary, Turgenev incorporated the scientific rational egotism of the nihilists within the world of the novel. By so doing, he turned a philosophical debate into a depiction of life as lived by individuals experiencing different meaningful versions of existence. We live ideas in specific settings with the character we have and with necessarily incomplete understanding of our own and others' motivations. Mikhail Bakhtin argued such complexity is where ethical thought becomes real. Abstract debates cannot serve as an alibi for not taking responsibility for the complexity of real human interaction between individuals (Bakhtin *Toward*). Turgenev's novel answers nihilism by confronting it with both human complexity and the ambiguous meaningfulness of life. Its value to a core course is that it forces us to do the same.

Works Cited

Bakhtin, Mikhail. *Problems of Dostoevsky's Poetics*. Trans. Caryl Emerson. Minneapolis: U of Minnesota, 1984.

———. *Toward a Philosophy of the Act*. Trans. Vadim Liapunov. Austin: U of Texas, 1993.

Berlin, Isaiah. "Fathers and Children: Turgenev and the Liberal Predicament." *Russian Thinkers*. New York: Penguin, 1994. 261–304.

Eldridge, Richard. *Literature, Life and Modernity*. New York: Columbia, 2008.

Ingarden, Roman. *The Literary Work of Art: An Investigation on the Borderlines of Ontology, Logic, and Theory of Literature*. Trans. George G. Grabowicz. Evanston: Northwestern, 1973.

Kundera, Milan. *The Art of the Novel*. Trans. Linda Asher. New York: Grove, 1986.

Nussbaum, Martha. *Not For Profit: Why Democracy Needs the Humanities*. Princeton: Princeton UP, 2010.

Turgenev, Ivan. *Fathers and Sons*. Trans. Rosemary Edmonds. Middlesex, UK: Penguin, 1965.

How to Illustrate Blind Ambition to a Business Student: Looking at the World through the Eyes of Dreiser's *Financier*

Vincent Rama
William Paterson University

Business ethics remains a tough sell. After all, the business world continues to declare itself to be a moral free zone. So, why should we expect our business students to take a course on business ethics seriously? If we stick to the compliance script and restrict our discussion of business ethics to rules and regulations, penalties and fines, our students, and our colleagues on the business school faculty, will tolerate what we have to say—deeming it to have at least some degree of real world relevance. Our students may even listen to the case studies we present and the legal precedents we refer to with measured interest. But we will not address the bifurcated existence of the contemporary business person whose life is disproportionately split between the values demanded by the workplace—profit, power, prestige—and the values demanded by the people in his life and the planet that he lives upon—compassion, care, and concern.

So how do we reach our business students? How do get across to them the importance of integrating working and non-working hours into a single experience, a single conscience in which they remain sensitive to the values of the fellow human beings and their planet? We tell them a story. We draw them into a story. Enter Frank Cowperwood, the main character in Theodore Dreiser's *The Financier*.

Dreiser employs the perspectives of both psychology and philosophy (perspectives which are out of bounds in our compliance-constricted business ethics courses) as he walks us through the rise and fall of Frank Cowperwood. The novelist exposes us to Cowperwood's worldview. He shows us his value system, his aspirations, and his dreams. He also lets us follow Cowperwood's behavior, his path from financial success and career advancement to greed, corruption, and lust. We see the subtle steps, the small transgressions, the bending of the rules that gradually becomes standard operating procedures. We see a life slowly and ever so slightly go off the rails. We see the house of cards patiently assembled.

This is the kind of story that shows us where a Bernie Madoff comes from. It takes us down the path by which a legitimate business person starts to cut corners, fabricate accounts, dupe customers, and treat co-workers as pawns. What does the world look like to a white-collar criminal? Does a warped worldview explain the immoral and criminal behavior, or does a pattern of minor transgressions aggregate into habitual malevolence, and gradually constitute the corrupt perspective? These are the questions that Dreiser explores in Frank Cowperwood's life.

We meet Frank as a bright young boy with a promising future. His first employer, Henry Waterman, tells his brother and partner, George, that this seventeen-year-old boy, Cowperwood, conveys "something easy and sufficient about him. He does not appear to be in the least flustered or disturbed" (Dreiser 23). The two brothers marvel at how quickly Frank picks up the bookkeeping of their complicated commodities business, and they begin to see him as an integral part of their company's future. But Frank has other ideas. As the two brothers present him with a five-hundred-dollar Christmas bonus, Frank is thinking about how inferior they are to him, and is planning to leave their employment as soon as the next opportunity presents itself. "These two men he worked for were already nothing more than characters in his eyes. . . . He could see their weakness and their shortcomings as much as a much older man might have viewed a boy's" (29).

As a teenager, Cowperwood is confident and efficient, a quick learner and an energetic worker. But he is also someone who at this young age is exposed to the readiness of people of power and wealth to make use of lesser people as pawns in their financial and political schemes. He admires the brokers at his second place of employment, Tighe and Company, for their psychological prowess—they know how to read their customers and their competition. They instinctively identify weakness and are always ready to pounce: "They were like hawks," Cowperwood tells us, "watching for an opportunity to snatch their prey from under the very claws of their opponents" (42). Yet as impressive as the brokers are, Frank sees them as mere instruments in the hands of even wealthier, more powerful people:

> As in the case of Waterman & Company, he sized up these men shrewdly, judging some to be weak, some foolish, some clever, some slow, but in the main all small-minded or deficient because they were agents, tools, or gamblers. A man, a real man, must never be an agent, a tool, or a gambler—acting for himself or others—he must employ such. A real man—a financier—was never a tool. He used tools. He created. He led. (44)

As Dreiser shows us how Frank develops a worldview that supports his business practices, he also shows us the actions that the financier takes, the behavior that reflects, justifies, and replenishes his metaphysical stance. We have already mentioned Frank's lack of concern with any loyalty that he might have been expected to display towards his first employers. When the opportunity was right, he was ready to move on. He shows the same lack of concern for commitment in his relationship with his first wife, Lillian. He shows no sense of guilt in courting her while she is married to another man; then he simply leaves her and their children behind when the younger, prettier Aileen Butler catches his attention. He states matter-of-factly: "Mrs. Cowperwood was no longer what she should be physically and mentally, and that in itself to him was sufficient to justify his present interest in this girl" (135).

When Cowperwood finally makes his move into clearly illegal and immoral activity, we are not surprised. Frank, like the brokers at Tighe &Company, is armed with the lethal combination of skill in manipulating markets and skill in manipulating people. Having numbed his conscience to any sense of evil or corruption in his actions, he is on the lookout for his opportunity to join the company of the rich and powerful inner circle of Philadelphia. Dreiser describes the amoral leaning of the "prowling" Cowperwood as follows:

> Cowperwood was an opportunist. And by this time his financial morality had become special and local in its character. He did not think it was wise for any one to steal anything from anybody where the act of taking or profiting was directly and plainly considered stealing. That was unwise—dangerous—hence wrong. There were so many situations wherein one might do in the way of taking or profiting was open to discussion and doubt. Morality varied, in his mind at least, with conditions, if not climates" (149).

Cowperwood finds the perfect opportunity and the perfect pawn in the person of George Stener, the Philadelphia City Treasurer. Cowperwood convinces Stener to let him use city funds for a stock market manipulation scheme. Cowperwood revels in the chance to finally make use of his financial skills on a grand scale:

> Imagine yourself by nature versed in the arts of finance, capable of playing with sums of money in the forms of stocks, certificates, bonds, and cash, as the ordinary man plays with checkers or chess. Or, better yet, imagine yourself one of those subtle master of the mysteries of the higher form of chess—the type of mind so well illustrated by the famous and historic chess-players, who could sit with their backs to a group of rivals playing fourteen men at once, calling out all the moves in turn, remembering all the positions of all the men on all the boards, and winning. (108)

The venture works out beautifully, and the two men use their profits to buy up shares of the promising streetcar lines that are springing up all over Philadelphia. All is good until the Chicago fire devastates the financial markets and exposes their scheme. At his trial, Cowperwood shows no remorse and offers no apologies. Dreiser describes the financier's attitude as follows: "He believed in the financial *rightness* of the thing he had done. He was entitled to it.... Why should he bother about petty, picayune minds which could not understand this" (345)?

Cowperwood's conviction and subsequent jail time have no rehabilitative effect. Dreiser does not provide the predictable morality tale that we are accustomed to. The novel ends with Cowperwood back on his feet financially, seizing the next great opportunity, making money once again. His sister comments on his return to prosperity with disbelief: "[S]he did not understand how justice and morals were arranged in this world. There seemed to be certain general principles—or people assumed there were—but apparently there were exceptions. Assuredly her brother abided by no known rule. and yet he seemed to be doing fairly well once more. What did this mean" (502)?

Dreiser leaves us pondering the role of his financier in the greater universe. This is the promise that using novels like this offers to teachers of business ethics. We follow this talented young man in his rapid rise to fame and fortune. we peer into his perspective on life. and we follow him through the decisions that cross the boundary lines of morality and legality. A case study does not give you the ability to see the world through another man's vision. nor does it give you access to the slow and subtle behavioral changes that accompany the corruption of a human conscience. Dreiser's novels do this as do other great works of literature.

As interesting as legal cases and precedents may be. they do not show conscience and character from the inside of a human being. No business student ever pictures himself or herself as the next great swindler on the front page of the newspaper. Dreiser pulls us into the account of a life that ends up this way. He presents the story of a brilliant, skilled. and driven worker whose life is focused upon establishing himself as a powerful and prestigious force. admired by his friends and feared by his enemies. Other people are his pawns and his tools. In his world. law is something manipulated by the people in power. Religion is the refuge of the weak. Art is a sign of prestige and success.

Dreiser forces us to acknowledge the life of Frank Cowperwood as a real possibility. This is why we need stories in our business ethics classrooms.

Work Cited

Dreiser, Theodore. *The Financier*. New York: Penguin Books. 2008.

Tayeb Salih's *Season of Migration to the North* and the Pathologies of Moral Philosophy

Irfan Khawaja
Felician College

Tayeb Salih (1929–2009) was a Sudanese novelist well-known in the Arabic-speaking world. and the author of some twenty-five important works of literature. all in Arabic. of which *Season of Migration to the North* is the best known. At one level the novel is an African author's re-working and re-telling of two European classics. Joseph Conrad's *Heart of Darkness* and Shakespeare's *Othello*. And yet *Season* is much more than a mere re-fashioning of great European classics. In acknowledgment of this. much of the secondary literature on *Season* focuses, justifiably. on what the novel has to say about the postcolonial predicament. interpreting its characters' depredations as a response to the pathologies of British imperialism, and ascribing to Salih himself the desire to "write back" at some of the classics of the Western literary canon. Without denying the legitimacy of that approach. I'd like to suggest that the book can also profitably be read as a contribution to the study of moral philosophy.

In pedagogical contexts. moral philosophers often insist. in the name of fairness. in presenting moral theories at their *best*—that is. in terms of the best arguments that might be given by an idealized advocate of the theory under discussion. But this (in some contexts laudable) aim overlooks the fact that theories are almost never practiced at their best. As a result, students of moral philosophy rarely grapple with the disconcerting gap that exists between idealized theories at their best and real-life expressions of those theories at their worst. Nor are they encouraged to pay much attention to possible connections between theory and practice: when theories fail. philosophers are often morbidly eager to blame practitioners for the failures (e.g..

Kant, *Grounding* 19–23, 58–62). By contrast, *Season* opens up the more disturbing possibility that the deepest defects may well lie in the theories themselves. In this connection, *Season* is, I suggest, usefully interpreted as a depiction of the pathologies that arise when ordinary people put high-minded theories into practice in a morally complex world. Implicitly, at least, the novel shows us how theories that lack the resources for self-correction in the face of complexity ultimately produce both tragedy and farce. In what follows, I illustrate this point on four theories commonly covered in introductory courses on moral philosophy—cultural relativism, deontology, ethical egoism, and utilitarianism.

Cultural relativism is the view that moral norms apply within but not across cultures. The analogy here is with language: just as the grammatical and syntactical rules of a language apply to that language but not to others, so by relativist strictures, the moral norms and judgments of a given culture apply to that culture but not to others. In other words, as the member of a given culture, I can sit in moral judgment of other members of *my* culture, but must profess agnosticism on the doings of alien cultures, however repulsive, degrading, or otherwise problematic they might seem to me.

So conceived, relativism doesn't get very good press in philosophy these days, but in cultural anthropology, where it was first formulated (and in postcolonial studies, where it was reformulated) relativism arose as a way of getting "Westerners" to show appropriate modesty in making cross-cultural judgments, and humility in implementing cross-cultural policies. On this view, relativism is an epistemological form of anti-racism and anti-imperialism: we should (it tells us) fear to tread where we lack the epistemological resources to know, and that means most places. But as has become obvious over the past few decades, taken literally, relativism is self-refuting, and often enough ends up as a rationalization for brutality and injustice. So understood, relativism doesn't merely "lead to" pathology; it *is* one (see Williams *Morality* 34–39, and Nussbaum 113–47).

It is hard to think of a novel that more directly and mercilessly throws the inadequacies of cultural relativism into relief than *Season*, a fact brought home by the novel's anonymous narrator. For one thing, the book's narrative forces the reader from the novel's first page to question the foundational dogma of cultural relativism, namely, the coherence of the idea of cultural membership itself. What the narrator shows us in vivid detail is the descriptive and explanatory inadequacy of the idea that any of us inhabit a single, uniform culture; it quickly becomes obvious that even the most tradition-bound member of the narrator's village is in fact a member of several different cultures at once. Having put cultural membership in doubt, the novel then demands that readers choose sides in an internecine quarrel *within* what at first appears to be a single culture. Ironically, it is the narrator, who, despite his nostalgic approval of ancient village norms, delivers the novel's most emphatic rejections of relativism, and who offers the most ferocious condemnations of "his people's" beliefs and behavior.

And one would have to be a dogmatist to disagree with him. For what we confront in the novel is a "culture" in which child rape, forced female circumcision, incest, slavery, serial marriage/divorce, and polygamy are all taken for granted, and rationalized in terms of opportunistically patriarchal interpretations of the Qur'an. To apply relativist strictures to these activities is of necessity to condemn the more assertive or rebellious (Sudanese) characters in the novel who oppose them; to sympathize with those characters is to fall out of sympathy for relativism. By ingeniously implicating the reader in intra-cultural conflict, *Season* makes the demand that readers acknowledge cultural diversity while taking a perspective on it that requires moral judgment of individuals as individuals. The result is a participatory dissection of the pathologies of cultural relativism that is more instructive than those usually offered in textbook discussions of the subject.

In rejecting relativism, we might be inclined to turn for an alternative to *deontology*, as expressed in the views of the arch anti-relativist in the history of ethics, Immanuel Kant (1724–1804). On Kant's view, deontology is the thesis that morality consists of a series of absolute prescriptions binding on all human beings regardless of cultural membership, performed for their own sake rather than from expectation of reward. Perhaps the most attractive feature of Kant's ethics is its uncompromising conception of rational agents as beings with infinite dignity, whose autonomy is categorically to be respected by treating them always as ends and never as mere means. The result is an ethics of non-coercion, non-exploitation, and non-manipulation, in which rational agents offer one another reasons for action, relying only on the verdicts of reason for acceptance or rejection of one another's proposals. An ethic further removed from relativism and from Sudanese village life can hardly be imagined.

And yet however attractive one finds Kant's anti-relativism, the Kantian vision has its own dark side, exemplified in the puritanical severities of Kant's moral psychology, according to which the "pathological" promptings of desire, self-love, happiness, and even self-knowledge are to be kept strictly subordinate to the relentless demands of duty.[1] One possible incarnation of this moral vision is the person fixated on duty to the point of repression—that is, the person who subconsciously drives his deepest desires underground for fear of discovering his moral verdicts on them. Another is the person who finds himself unable to give determinate content to Kant's (very abstract) conception of duty, and so conflates Kantian morality with the conventional conceptions of duty unthinkingly inherited from his social milieu.

Both incarnations find expression, once again, in the book's narrator. On the one hand, what strikes us about him is the tumultuous and notably unKantian character of his internal life: his deep and nostalgic sense of filial attachment and rootedness, his moral and political cynicism, his intense romantic yearnings, and his sincere (if sporadic) *joie de vivre*. On the other hand, when it comes to action, what becomes painfully clear is the extent to which the same person is governed by a moral conception that is a caricature of the robotically dutiful Kantian. Thus, under the right conditions, our unKantian narrator becomes the kind of person who abandons a loved one to a foreseeable death in order to uphold a relatively trivial set of promises (cf. Kant's *Supposed Right* 63–65). The result is a schizophrenic self, whose two unintegrated halves are hidden from one another by a self-deceived fixation on Duty, conventionally understood. This schizophrenic self may well be a perversion of Kantian ethics, but even so, the novel forces us to reckon with the ways in which Kantian ethics encourages those perversions. and thereby raises questions about the resources that Kantians have for correcting them.

Suppose that we correct for Kant's rigorism by insisting that pleasure and personal happiness ought to play a larger role in ethical life than Kant allows. If we take this insistence far enough. we may want to insist that morality make an active and consistent contribution to the happiness of its practitioners. and thus be led to a form of *ethical egoism*. Ethical egoism is the view that every moral agent ought to be the ultimate intended beneficiary of his or her own actions.[2] Put more simply, egoism is the thesis that each of us ought to act in our self-interest, so that every act a person undertakes aims primarily to benefit that person, whoever else it benefits along the way.

There are and have always been both benign and malign versions of this view. The benign versions involve an optimistic conception of the self's interests. so that self-interest requires a commitment to moral virtues like honesty, integrity, and justice (see, e.g., Smith). The malign versions. by contrast. leave our self-interest elastically undefined. giving us license to do as we please. however destructive to others. Even if one accepts the benign versions of egoism. however. it's clear that in practice. the motive of self-interest can come into conflict with the impartiality and other-regard we justifiably expect of one another. and a benign egoism that fails to make provision for this fact can easily lapse into malignance.

Everything we learn about the novel's *other* protagonist. Mustapha Sa'eed. exemplifies a radically malign egoism—habitual dishonesty. self-worship. ingratitude, misogyny. malice, and a ruthless will to power. A character who combines immorality and self-interest in this way raises two fundamental challenges for egoism as a theory. For one thing. how is he to be condemned on egoistic grounds? In what way does this egoist *not* achieve his self-interest? Second. is there anything in egoism that is itself conducive to the formation of such a person?

The novel does not. of course. directly answer these questions. but it gives us the material with which to begin an answer. What is remarkable are the specifically theoretical ingredients of the egoism it depicts. As it turns out. Mustapha Sa'eed is an academic who collects foreign books as Conrad's Kurtz collects native skulls (Said 211). and his self-descriptions. however morbid. are often remarkably bookish. involving both covert and overt references to Plato, Nietzsche. and Freud—all three of them theorists of egoism. Though Plato. Nietzsche. and Freud would undoubtedly disown the likes of Mustapha Sa'eed. what is of interest to the student of moral philosophy are the glimpses of their theories. however distorted. that we see in him. What the novel shows us. at last. is the *sort of self* whose desires could corrupt even the most benign form of egoism—a demonstration. I think. that provides more insight into egoism than standard textbook "refutations" of the doctrine.

Someone disenchanted with egoism might be inclined to retain its focus on happiness but change its focus on the self. Perhaps the problem with egoism is its too insistent focus on one's *own* happiness at the expense of others. In that case. perhaps egoism is to be remedied by appeal to *utilitarianism*. which prescribes a heavy dose of altruistic concern for the good of others. Utilitarianism. as Bentham's slogan has it. is the thesis that we ought to promote "the greatest happiness for the greatest number." calculating this happiness so that each individual is regarded impartially as counting for one and none counts for more than one.[3] The result is a sort of egalitarian impartialism in which instead of putting our own interests first, we self-consciously subordinate them to "the permanent interests of man as a progressive being" (Mill 16). Unfortunately, as Bernard Williams and others have pointed out, there is, alongside this sunny moral conception, also a darker "Government House" version of utilitarianism, with its cavalier rationalizations for power, and its problematic complicities with imperialism (Williams, *Ethics and the Limits* 108–10; see also Schultz and Varouxakis).

Like relativism but unlike egoism and Kantianism, utilitarianism is not expressed by any single character in the novel, but forms its backdrop as such. Though chronologically, *Season*'s plot proceeds from the Sudan to Britain and back via Cairo, there is a sense in which the plot operates in a single (British) imperial culture, whose official stance derives, directly or indirectly, from the traditions of English utilitarianism. The very fact of a British imperial system encompassing the Sudan owes its existence in part to the utilitarian imperative to do good in the world (and to benefit from that do-gooding), and the implicit paternalism and racial condescension involved in this project are never far from the novel's surface.

In mirror-image, utilitarianism finds perverse and ironic expression in Mustapha Sa'eed's professional life as an anti-imperialist economist. His books—*The Economics of Colonialism, Colonialism and Monopoly, The Cross and Gunpowder, The Rape of Africa, Prospero and Caliban*—all hold the British to their own egalitarian standards and find them wanting (the irony being that after writing them, Sa'eed is himself judged a murderer in an English court of law). And then there are the various minor characters, both Sudanese and English, who crop up in the guise of academic and bureaucratic busybodies, all of them with bright-eyed schemes for the salvation of the new postcolonial Sudan. One particularly vivid example is Mahjoub, Chairman of the village's Agricultural Project Committee, whose obsessions with collective welfare and power blind him to the life-and-death dramas being enacted before his own eyes. Another is Richard, an English hold-over in the Ministry of Finance, who—in a particularly sanctimonious lecture to a Sudanese audience—makes a self-contradictory argument for value-neutrality in economics, thereby exposing the incoherence of the work he ostensibly does for the good of his Sudanese wards.

The common denominator of the utilitarians in *Season*—imperialist or anti-imperialist, English or Sudanese—is the strange kinship that their "respectable" views bear to the "Satanic" egoism of the novel's most transparently evil character, Mustapha Sa'eed. Like Sa'eed, they believe that human lives are mere instruments of the will of those with the power to instrumentalize them. Unlike Sa'eed, they are deluded into believing that their will to power is the epitome of virtue.

What, then, is the upshot of our exercise? At first glance, it might seem as though Salih's novel has a purely negative or deconstructive role to play in ethical pedagogy and inquiry, for in each case *Season* seems to do little more than to underscore the failures of the ethical theories that students commonly encounter in a survey class. If we add to these failures the more theoretical objections to the theories discussed in textbooks, it's natural to worry that the use of *Season* as a core text in moral philosophy might abet the cynicism, skepticism, or outright nihilism that undergraduates bring to class on their own.

There is, no doubt, a real danger here. But there is, in my view, a greater danger involved in conventional approaches to pedagogy in moral philosophy, which leave students with theories so artificially abstracted from real life as to bear no discernible relation to the lives that flesh-and-blood people might actually lead. *Season* introduces a complexity into moral philosophy that makes for messy pedagogical dynamics, but in so doing, pays tribute to the complexity of the world that moral philosophy is supposed to address. The great merit of Salih's novel is to force us to look more directly and without evasion at that complexity, and to make the attempt to grapple with it a permanent endeavor.[4]

Notes

1. On happiness, see Kant's *Grounding* (8–17, 46), *Practical Reason* (20–24, 53–56, 60–75, 103–4), and *Religion* (5–7n, 22, 41n, 61, 69n, 125, 130, 149ff). On self-knowledge, see *Grounding* (19–20) and *Metaphysics of Morals* (236, 241–42, 271). On desire, see *Grounding* (24, 59n.3).

2 Thanks to Allan Gotthelf for this succinct formulation.

3 The quoted phrase is from Bentham's *Principles*, notes 1 and 4 of chapter 1 (1, 5). The calculational principle, often attributed to Bentham as though it were a direct quotation, is in fact a formulaic summary of the counting procedure described in *Principles* IV.5.6 (31).

4 Thanks to my students in Introduction to Ethics (John Jay College) and General Ethics (Felician College) for many illuminating insights into Salih's novel, and especially to Ryan Nardi for insight into the specifically literary merits of the book. Thanks also to Carrie-Ann Biondi for hours of discussion about Season, and for substantive and editorial comments on a draft of this essay.

Works Cited

Bentham, Jeremy. 1781. *Principles of Morals and Legislation*. Amherst, NY: Prometheus Books, 1988.

Kant, Immanuel. 1788. *Critique of Practical Reason*. Ed. Mary Gregor, Intro. Andrews Reath. New York: Cambridge UP, 1997.

———. *Grounding for the Metaphysics of Morals*. 1785. Trans. James W. Ellington. Indianapolis: Hackett Publishing Company, 1993.

———. *The Metaphysics of Morals*. 1797. Trans. Mary Gregor. New York: Cambridge UP, 1991.

———. *On a Supposed Right to Lie Because of Philanthropic Concerns* (Supplement to *Grounding for the Metaphysics of Morals*). 1799. Trans. James W. Ellington. Indianapolis: Hackett Publishing Company, 1993.

———. *Religion Within the Limits of Reason*. 1793. Trans. Theodore M. Greene and Hoyt H. Hudson. New York: Harper and Bros., 1960.

Mill, J. S. "On Liberty." 1859. *Three Essays*. Ed. Richard Wollheim. Oxford: Oxford UP, 1975.

Nussbaum, Martha C. *Cultivating Humanity: A Classical Defense of Reform in Liberal Education*. Cambridge: Harvard UP, 1997.

Said, Edward W. *Culture and Imperialism*. New York: Vintage Books, 1993.

Salih, Tayeb. *Season of Migration to the North*. Trans. Denys Johnson-Davies. Intro. Laila Lalami. New York: New York Review Books, 2009.

Schultz, Bart and Georgios Varouxakis. Eds. *Utilitarianism and Empire*. Lanham, MD:Lexington Books, 2005.

Smith, Tara. *Ayn Rand's Normative Ethics: The Virtuous Egoist*. New York: Cambridge UP, 2006.

Williams, Bernard. *Ethics and the Limits of Philosophy*. Cambridge: Harvard UP, 1985.

———. *Morality: An Introduction to Ethics*. Harmondsworth, UK: Penguin Books, 1972.